Thomas Miller

The Poetical Language of Flowers

The pilgrimage of love. Fifth Edition

Thomas Miller

The Poetical Language of Flowers
The pilgrimage of love. Fifth Edition

ISBN/EAN: 9783337816278

Printed in Europe, USA, Canada, Australia, Japan

Cover: Foto ©Andreas Hilbeck / pixelio.de

More available books at **www.hansebooks.com**

LANGUAGE OF FLOWERS.

THE

POETICAL LANGUAGE OF FLOWERS;

OR,

The Pilgrimage of Love.

BY

THOMAS MILLER.

"A book,
In which thou wilt find many a lovely saying
About the leaves and flowers,—about the playing
Of nymphs in woods and fountains, and the shade
Keeping a silence round a sleeping maid."—KEATS.

FIFTH EDITION.

LONDON:
GRIFFIN, BOHN, AND COMPANY,
STATIONERS' HALL COURT.
MDCCCLXII.

LONDON:

T. HARRILD, PRINTER, SHOE LANE,

FLEET STREET.

Dedication

TO THE PRINCESS ROYAL OF ENGLAND.

Rosebud of England! I have chosen thee
From all the beauties of the flowery train
Sole Princess o'er this rainbow-realm to reign:
Through all the land none worthier can I see,
Beyond the shadow of the royal tree,
To sway the sceptre o'er this sweet domain;
Subjects that perfume hill, and vale, and plain,
Wherever sings the bird or hums the bee.
I bring before thee England's choicest posies.
Dappled like her own skies at Day's first hours,
Almost as beautiful as thine own roses:
I've gathered them for thee in woodland bowers,
Where the bud opens and the blossom closes,
That thou may'st reign over this Land of Flowers.

Thomas Miller.

PREFACE.

All the books which have hitherto treated on the Language of the Flowers are, with the exception of a few slight alterations and additions, mere translations from the French work of Aimé Martin; nor am I aware of any production in the English language on this subject which professes to be original, saving the present. If flowers, the most beautiful objects in nature, are to be converted into the messengers of friendship and love, and are capable of conveying beautiful and poetical meanings, it is surely worth while to trace a resemblance between the flower and the emblem it represents, which shall, at least, have some show of reason in it. This task I have attempted, taking for my guides no less authorities than Chaucer, Spenser, Shakspeare, and Milton; whatever meanings they have attributed to the flowers I have retained, and also endeavoured, like them, to find, in either the name or the nature of the flower, some resemblance to the thought it is intended to express, and so, by adding here and there a blossom to the beautiful wreath they have left unfinished, I trust that I have done something towards the completion of a work which shall be worthy of the name of England's Language of Flowers.

In the legends which illustrate each sentiment, or group of flowers, I have endeavoured to create a new interest, by linking them with human affections and fanciful narratives, the origin of which may either be traced in the old heathen writers, or found amid the lighter lore of our own day. Not that I have fettered myself to any given rules, or chained my fancy to any circumscribed space; for I will not yet believe that there is

> "So small a range
> In the present strength of manhood, that the high
> Imagination cannot freely fly,
> As she was wont of old;"

but that she can, as in former days, spread out her free wings when she listeth, and

> "Show us all,
> From the clear space of ether to the small
> Breath of new buds unfolding:"

for I have more faith in the love of my country for the old fanciful literature, than many have.

To me England has ever been an island "full of sweet sounds that give delight and hurt not:" and I think that a nation so rich in poetry as ours, should not be without its own Language of Flowers. Better believe in the messages the bees brought from the flowers on Mount Hymettus, when they settled upon the lips of Plato, and foretold that there slept the eloquence which would one day charm the world; or endeavour to trace fanciful letters in the wavy lines and mazy forms which they sometimes assume, as they streak the green hill-side, than find in them no meaning at all—that the blossoms still send tidings abroad, which when once whispered into the ear settle down noiselessly into the hearts of all who believe in the poetry, and beauty, and love of the flowers.

Although my Index of the emblematic meanings of the flowers varies considerably from that which is appended to the French work before referred to, still I doubt not that it will be found more accurate, and that the reasons I have given for adopting the emblems attached to the flowers are clearer and more comprehensive than any that have hitherto appeared. In every floral index which I have seen, the Meadow-sweet, or

Queen of the Meadows, is made the emblem of Uselessness: a sweeter flower does not blow; it is only equalled by the blossoms of the Hawthorn in perfume, and I think I have with good reason changed its signification to Neglected Beauty. Again, the Anemone, or Wind-flower of the Greeks, has been selected as the emblem of Forsaken Love: I have, in honour of Milton, chosen the Primrose; for the Bard of Paradise has beautifully said,—

"The rathe Primrose that forsaken dies;"

and we seldom see one bud alone on the root. So have I gone on through all my fanciful or poetical illustrations: either following the old poets, or gathering from the very nature of the flower some quality that represents the sentiment I have attached to it. The subject has never before been taken up in the old poetical spirit: there are signs of a timid step and trembling hand, which betray a want of confidence in the task, as if it had not been a labour of love. I have proceeded without fear, and have adapted many "an old-world story" to the meanings of the flowers, which, I trust, will give pleasure to all my readers.

T. M.

CONTENTS.

LIST OF PLATES.

DRAWN AND COLOURED BY JAMES ANDREWS.

TIME, LOVE, AND THE FLOWERS.

Said Time, "I cannot bear the flowers,
 They spoil the look of old decay;
They cover all my ruined towers,
 My fallen shrines, and abbeys grey:
I'll cut them down—why should they grow?
 I marvel Death upon his graves
Allows so many buds to blow!
 O'er all my works the Wallflower waves!"—
His scythe he sharpened as he spoke,
And deeper frowned at every stroke.

In vain did Beauty him entreat
 To spare the flowers, as on the ground
She weeping knelt, and clasped his feet.
 He only turned his head half round,

And sternly bade her go her way.
  Said Time, "Were all the world to plead
They should not live another day,
  No, not if Death did intercede!"—
He took his scythe and at one sweep
The flowers became a withered heap.

Time came again, and so did Spring;
  The spot once more with flowers was strown,
He scarce could see a ruined thing,
  So tall and thick the buds had grown.
"Oh, oh!" said Time, "I must upturn,
  Dig deep, and cover in like Death;
I'll not leave one behind to mourn,
  Or sweeten more the breeze's breath:
Full fathom five I'll lay them low,
Then leave them if they can to grow!"

Summer met Time in that same place,
  It looked more lovely than of old,
For there had sprung another race
  Of flowers from out the upturned mould,
Which had been buried long ago.
  "How's this?" said Time, and rubbed his eyes.
"I have laid many a city low,
  But never more saw turret rise."—
Love at that moment chanced to pass,
He touched Time's arm, and shook his glass.

"Old man," said Love, "the flowers are mine;
Leave them alone, and go thy way—
Destruction is the work of thine,
'Tis mine to beautify decay.
Is 't not enough that thou hast power
To lay both youth and beauty low,
But thou must envy the poor flower
Which scarce a day sees in full blow?
I've seen thee smile on them for hours!"—
"'T is true," said Time, and spared the flowers.

THE

LANGUAGE OF FLOWERS.

LOVE AND THE FLOWERS.

Upon a bed of roses Love reclined,
The heart-dyed flowers across his mouth were thrown,
And both their sweets were in one breath combined,
As if they from the self-same bud had blown;
You could not tell, so sweetly were they blended,
Where swelled Love's crimson lip, nor where the rose-bloom ended.

IT was in that age, when the golden mornings of the early world were unclouded by the smoke of cities; when the odours from thousands of untrodden flowers mingled with the aroma of old forests, and the gentlest wind that ever tried its wings flapped its way through vast realms of sleeping fragrance—that Love first set out to discover the long-lost Language of the Flowers. There had long been rumours in the olden world, that before the angels left their watch beside the star-beaconed battlements of Heaven, and gave up all their glory for the love of woman, the Buds and Blossoms had held sweet converse together; and that many a time when the nightingale ushered in the twilight with her song, voices from the flowers had made low response amongst the glades and rose-girded pastures of the Garden of Paradise. Even on Olympus, Love had heard that an immortal language never could die; that, although silent, it still slept somewhere amongst the flowers. And many a time, whilst resting on some fragrant bed, he had been awakened by low whisperings, and disturbed by the heavy beating of his heart, which ever seemed urging him onward to commence his holy mission, and discover that language, which had been lost ever since the day when Eve went weeping from beneath the angel-guarded gates of Eden.

Love arose, and shook the rounded dew in loosened pearls from the feathery silver of his wings, and soared far away over many a hill and valley; alighting when weary, and kneeling lowly, with attentive ear and bowed head, beside the blossoms. For a long time he only learnt what the bees said when they hung murmuring over the honeyed bells, and what words the butterflies whispered as they alighted upon the flowers with subsiding wings. Onward wandered Love for many a day;—although he caught the faint breathing of the blossoms, yet the meaning of their lowest words was still to him a mystery. At last, weary and sad at heart, he sat down and wept upon a bed of roses. The Rose was his mother's favourite flower, it had ever been sacred to Venus, and he heard a sound, as of low sighing, amongst its leaves; and when he laid down, he felt the drooping petals falling upon his lips and around his neck, as if to catch the tears that fell. Then it was that Love first kissed the Rose and blessed it unawares, for the sweetness and beauty of the flower sank into his heart. Whilst folded upon his lips, she told him, that ages ago Jove selected her for the Queen of Flowers and the Goddess of Beauty; that nothing human had ever surpassed her charms: and that when every image of poetry was exhausted, none could equal her own; that from the first creation of flowers, she had been named "the ornament of the earth, the princess of plants, the eye of the flower, the blush of beauty, the breath of love."* That even when her leaves had withered, to mark her immortal origin, she gave not up her breath, but still lived in a spirit of invisible fragrance; that she never knew old age, but sank to sleep in perfume, in the full perfection of her beauty, for she was the fairest daughter that

* Fragment attributed to Sappho.

was born of the Mother of Love. So Love found his sweet and long-lost sister in the Rose, and she first spoke to him in the old language of the flowers, giving him a new lesson every day; until not a bell bowed, nor a bud expanded, nor a blossom opened its beautiful lips, but what Love knew every word it whispered.

For days did Love linger with his sweet sister, the Rose, before he again set out on his pilgrimage; but his journey was now no longer lonely; he found a companion in every flower by the wayside, and held converse with every bud that dwelt within its green homestead of leaves. The Honeysuckle told him how, in the olden age, she was the emblem of Devoted Affection; how she twined over rural and primeval huts, when love alone was counted happiness and the only wealth man coveted was the possession of a true heart—one that loved for evermore, and, throughout all the changes of time, for ever remained the same. The Lily blushed as he drew near, and across her pearly whiteness stole a crimson shadow, as if a winged rose had hovered above her for a moment, and then passed on; and with downcast eyes she told him, that to her belonged Purity of Heart; that she was once so holy a sanctuary, that even angels had deigned to dwell with her, and in their love for so spotless an abode had forfeited the domains of Heaven. The

Forget-me-not uplifted her blue eyes as he approached, and said, that she had never forgotten him, but had waited in patience and silence many an age for his coming; that, although her lips were sealed, she held fond communion with her own heart, and that she never looked up to the stars but they bade her hope; that she was still as true to Love as the blue heaven that bent over her, when first the morning-stars sang together for joy. The timid Violet shrank amid her broad leaves as she heard the approaching flutter of his wings; and long did Love linger around her, and sigh as he hung over her beauty: at last, she looked up and told him, that her home was the abode of Modesty; that she seldom ventured forth into the world; that those who loved her sought out her solitude, for she coveted not the gaze of a stranger's eye, nor loved to parade her beauty abroad amongst the blossoms; for there were those amongst the children of men who, forgetful of all modesty, peeped under her face, and looked into her downcast eyes. The Daisies rose up to welcome him, and gathered together in thousands to witness his approach. They made him a couch of their starry coronets, they embraced him with their green arms, and looked fondly upon him with their golden eyes, as they told him, in sweet, unstudied syllables, that they were the daughters of Innocence; and as Love gazed tenderly upon them, he felt a hushed and holy awe about his heart, such as had never touched those innocent flowers, that for ever remain in their childhood. Filled with sad and pleasing Thoughts, which gathered around him whilst he slept beside a bed of Pansies, he awoke and winged his way to a grey, old, ruined fortress, thinking that he there might ponder over the lessons he had learnt from the flowers. But on the mouldering battlements he beheld the wild Wall-flowers blowing; and when he inquired, why they still haunted such a scene of decay and desolation? they answered, that they had outlived all that was once lovely and happy; and although Beauty no longer reigned there, and the banquet-hall was deserted, and the voice of the lute had ceased to sound in the lady's bower—they were still Faithful amid all the storms of Adversity.

Long did Love brood over the new language which he had discovered, and many a day did he sit pondering to himself, as if hesitating whether or not he should trust Woman with the secret. "She is already armed with beauty," reasoned Love, as he sat with his elbow pillowed on a bed of flowers, his bow unstrung, and his arrows scattered at random by his side; "there is a language in her eyes, and a sweet music in her voice, and shall I now teach her to converse through flowers—to give a tongue to the rose, a voice to the lily, and hang upon the honeysuckle words of love, and turn every blossom she gathers into the language of affection? No; I will again fly abroad, and dropping a bud here, and a bell there, see to what purpose she turneth these beautiful secrets. I will but at first teach her a few letters in this new Alphabet of Love."

Then he thought, that as the flowers were such holy things—born of beauty and nursed in purity, fed upon the dews, and seldom looking upon aught less sacred than the stars, as if they were more allied to heaven than to earth—that if the virtue, and goodness, and love, which they represent, were but practised by mankind, they would again make the children of earth what they were in the infancy of the world, and man would once more be ranked "only a little lower than the angels."

Love flew to the burning East, where Beauty is guarded by jealous lattices, and Pride, armed with sharp scimitar, stands always ready, feeling its cold, keen edge, and waiting to cut every heart-sprung affection asunder; to punish a fond look unaccompanied by wealth, with death; and to dig a grave for every hallowed feeling that is unattended by Power. Love dropped a few flowers in the guarded turret and then concealed himself. A white hand shaped them after the fond feelings of her heart, and then extended her rounded arm and let them fall from the airy balcony ; and the lowly lover, who waited below, gathered up the banded flowers, and placing them upon his heart bore them away. He wept, mused, sighed, and smiled over them in his solitude, until he found their hidden meaning, and spelled out, letter by letter, the mysterious language of love. Fearlessly did he approach with them in his hand—he looked not, he spoke not: the watchful guardian smiled grimly upon his drawn scimitar, believing that its sharp edge had cut asunder every cord of love; for he saw not the bright eyes that peeped out from every bud—he beheld not the sweet lips that bent forward from every blossom. He heard not the language which the flowers uttered, and he saw not how Love looked on and smiled, as he noted every word which went back, and sank unperceived into the heart.

Ages passed away before Love entered the flowery fields and velvet valleys of merry England; his heart had long been light, and his wings unfettered, and he cared not now into what quarter of the world he wandered, for he found that wherever he went upon his flowery errand, man grew more refined, and woman each day bore a closer resemblance to the angels. The dinted helmet, the battered shield, and keen-pointed spear, were laid aside, and instead of rushing upon his mailed adversary, the warrior now sat a captive at the feet of Beauty. He visited ancient castles and humble hamlets, and thronged thorpes and thatched granges, and taught everywhere this new language of love. If he saw a rustic maiden with her head hanging aside, and her hands clasped, he plucked the fragrant blossom of the Hawthorn, and throwing it at her feet, whispered into her ear and bade her hope. As his foot dashed away the dew from the up-coned Lilac, he gathered the topmost sprig and threw it at her unsuspecting lover, who from that moment dated his first Emotions of Love. He pointed out the spot where many a blue-belled flower grew, and there they met and vowed to be Constant unto Death; and while they sat hand-in-hand gazing upon the white Water-Lilies that rested upon their thrones of green velvet, and were rocked by every ripple which curled the clear crystal of the lake, they felt that deep heaving of the heart which ever proclaimeth the Purity of Love.

So he wandered along;—and on wild moorlands, where rude huts rose, and scarce a flower broke the dark-brown solitude, Love left the broad Fern as a token of Sincerity: on bleak mountain-tops, where scarcely a tree threw down its chequered shadow to form a golden network upon the greensward, he planted the Harebell, and the crimson Heather, to give a charm to Retirement and Solitude. Into the depths of the loneliest woods he went, visiting deep dells and deserted dingles, where the graceful Lilies-of-the-Valley grew, telling them they were not forgotten, but should yet be proudly worn in many a fond breast that sighed for a Return of Happiness. Beside the Marigold, which closed its eyes as if for very Sorrow, he planted the Celandine, and leaving the Hawthorn, Hope, to cheer them and keep watch, he promised that, whilst ever the golden star shone there, it should be the image of Joys to Come. From flower to flower he flew on his peaceful pilgrimage: through them reconciling lovers who had long been estranged, and bringing back many a wandering affection that had often sighed for a fond heart to dwell within.

Thus Love restored a language which, for undated centuries, had been lost,—which the sweet tongue of woman had made music of before the beauty of the early world was submerged beneath the waters. For Time had all but blotted out the few records which told that there ever existed a language between Love and the Flowers.

Amid the broken and crumbling ruins over which Time has marched, he has only left the sculptured capital of some column, or shattered pedestal, where we can trace, among a hundred rude hieroglyphics, the rough outline of some flower, which was either sacred to their religion or their love. In the ruins of temples, whose origin even Antiquity has forgotten, we see in the life-like marble of the figures, brows which are wreathed with blossoms, and in the broken fresco we find groups of maidens strewing the pathway which leads to the holy shrine with flowers,—the carven altar is piled high with them, they garland the neck of the victim which their priests are about to sacrifice,—and, we know no more. Ages have passed away since that procession moved—the shadows of three thousand years have settled down over the hills and valleys, where those beautiful maidens first gathered the flowers of Summer,—history has left no record of their existence—the language in which they breathed their loves, their hopes, and their fears, has died away—even their name as a nation is forgotten: and all we know is, that their men looked noble, and their women beautiful, and that flowers were used in their sacred ceremonies, and that all, excepting the mute figures upon the marble, have long since passed away. We sigh, and try in vain to decipher these ancient emblems.

Love turned to the fables of the Heathen Poets, and there he found that those whose beauty the gods could not lift into immortality, they changed into flowers; as if they considered that, next to the glory of being enthroned upon Olympus, was to be transformed into a beautiful and fragrant object; one that, while as the sun shone upon the world, and the globed dews hung their rounded silver upon the blossoms, so long should it stand throughout all time,

"A thing of beauty and a joy for ever."

FORGET-ME-NOT.

LOVE, FORGET ME NOT, FOR IF FORSAKEN I DIE.

EMBLEMS.

LOVE, FORGET-ME-NOT—*MYRTLE:* FORSAKEN—*ANEMONE:* I DIE IF NEGLECTED—*LAURUSTINUS.*

Thy very name is Love's own Poetry,
  Born of the heart and of the eye begot,
Nursed amid sighs and smiles by Constancy,
  And ever breathing, "Love, Forget me not."

LOVE and flowers caused the wise king of Israel to break forth into song, and the lays he chanted to the dark-haired daughter of Egypt are amongst the richest notes that ever hung upon the golden chords of the lyre. That the divinity he adored was a fair daughter of Eve, whose beautiful form often glided through the fretted chambers of the princely palace of Jerusalem, even our most learned and grave commentators have been compelled to acknowledge: showing that the language in which we express our admiration of the matchless loveliness of woman, approaches so near our imperfect utterance of the adoration of heaven, that it is Love which first teaches us to lisp the holier thoughts that are wafted upward, and on the wings of prayer borne to the abode of the angels. In what a sea of bliss must the heart of the monarch have floated when, looking out from his casement over the green gardens of Jerusalem, he saw the whole landscape steeped in sunshine, as if thrown back and reflected from a mirror of gold; and gently awaking his beautiful and dark-eyed Egyptian bride, he breathed into her ear a sweet lay of love,—told her that the flowers had again appeared on the earth, that the singing-birds had returned from distant climes, and the voice of the turtle was heard in the land,—that the grapes threw out a sweet smell, and the young roes were feeding ámongst the lilies. He bade her come forth and show her beauty, like an apple-tree in full blossom amid the greenery of the surrounding woods. While he murmured in her ear, and placed his left hand under her head, and she looked back upon him with half-averted eyes;—the banner that waved over him was Love. He led her forth by the hand, and as her sable tresses blew back in the morning breeze, her queenly scarf streamed in an arch, like a rainbow, "backward borne," and she came down into the garden with a dancing step, skipping along in the very fulness of her love, like a young roe upon the mountains. Her lips were like a thread of scarlet, her neck like a stately tower, her hair like the floating silk of Cashmere; her teeth white and beautiful as a flock of lambs returning from the washing; her eyes, now and then hidden by the raven ringlets which blew across her queenly brow, were softer than the eyes of the dove when it bends over and coos to its young. As they walked along, a smell of spikenard, and cinnamon, and myrrh, perfumed the air; and as he gathered flowers, and placed them in her hand, he called her his garden—his delight: the sweetest blossom that ever hung over, or was reflected in the Nile, or opened beneath the earliest sunbeam that ever gilded the summits of her father's pyramids. They rambled onward through the garden of nuts—through the valley covered with myrtles, that evergreen emblem of Love, where the tendrils of the vine swayed idly in the morning air, and the pomegranates put forth their buds; they went far away among the pleasant fields, and, throwing aside their regal dignity, rested themselves amongst the homely villagers. He told her how Love is stronger than Death—that the wide waters which overflow Egypt would be unable to quench it; and that while he slept, his heart was still awake, and that his dreams were ever of Love.

Although the Myrtle is consecrated to Venus, and formed the garland with which the Goddess of Love and Beauty was crowned, growing also around the temples which were dedicated to her worship, still its antiquity dates not so far back as the Forget-me-not, which is as old as memory, and coeval with the creation of man. It was amongst the first flowers that sprang up from the saturated earth, after the overwhelming waters of the great deluge had subsided. Its history is found in the earliest records of the world, and woven with those legends which were current amongst the builders of Babel, who, in their ambition, attempted to rear a tower, the summit of which was to reach to the stars. Thousands of the traditions, that were rich in the lore of the antediluvian world, have been lost for ages, and it is only in those countries which were first peopled by the sons and daughters of Noah, that we are able to trace the faint outline of their origin, and in one of these relics of forgotten poetry we find the legend of the Forget-me-not.

It was on the site of one of those old homes of the early world—one that had stood beside the banks, where as beautiful a river flowed as had ever flashed back the golden lines of sunlight from the moving mirror of its waters—that a lost angel sat down, sad and sorrowful; his face buried in the palms of his hands, his long ringlets, which the celestial air of heaven had many a time fanned, drooped negligently over his rounded shoulders; and his broad white wings, which fell folded upon his back, looked as if they had borne the brunt of many a storm, and shaken from their white plumes the blinding rain of many a descending shower. He was one of those who had lost heaven through the love of woman, and had floated long days in the solitary air, his own image the only moving thing shadowed in the silent waters that covered the earth, while all below, excepting the ark, was buried beneath the deep deluge. He had seen the last fair face upturned on the high mountain-summit, supplicating Mercy, the last white hands raised and clasped in prayer, the dark locks floating upon the boiling foam, where the big rain danced down, and had poised himself like a voiceless bird above the desolation, for she who loved to watch him alight, the merciless eddies had borne far, far away for ever. But the waters had now subsided, the green hills had bared their tall summits, and the outstretched plains at their feet were once more visible. The top of many a mountain had now been washed away, and the fields which before waved with a thousand flowers were deeply covered beneath a new soil—the grave of all that was lovely and beautiful amongst women. And she, whose loss the angel mourned, whose image had so often floated between him and heaven, rising before his eyes when he stood with bowed head amid the ranged ranks of the winged cherubim, while the remembered echoes of her voice still seemed to sound upon his ears, and made the holy anthem which pealed through the vaulted gold grate like harsh music,—she, too, was buried deep below: the loveliest flower which the deluge had destroyed, amid all its wreck of bright and beautiful blossoms.

He raised the dim starlight of his eyes and gazed around, but not a vestige remained behind to tell of what had been. The trellised bower, over which, even at noonday, a green kind of shadowy twilight seemed to hang, was swept away, and not a trace left to mark out the spot where it had once stood. Groaning, he threw himself upon his side, and his great immortal heart beat as if it would have burst, while the snowy whiteness of his plumes was dabbled over with the dark soil, which had settled down and blotted out the light of her beauty whom he loved. "Never more," exclaimed he, in the utterance of his deep agony, "shall I lean upon thy warm shoulder in the evening sunset, listening to those silver accents, which to me were sweeter music, than that which floated through the envied heaven I have lost. Never more will those milk-white arms embrace me, nor shall I again taste the kisses which steeped the rounded roses of thy matchless lips, far sweeter than the dews which swell the pouting blossoms that blow in the immortal gardens above. Those golden ringlets which hung upon the downy whiteness of my wings, like the last deep rays of sunset shed over a bed of lilies, have now blended their bright clusters with the clod of the valley: those eyes, which but to look on made the stars, that pave the azure floor of that heaven which I shall never again tread, look dull, and dead, and rayless, will never again uplift their fringed curtains, and show the deep blue orbs, which swam in a sea of silver — they, alas! have closed their soft and melting brightness for ever. That heart, which was a fitting sanctuary for the Holy One Himself to dwell in, is now cold, and hushed, and motionless, and dark as the chaos I flew over at His bidding, long before the first morning broke upon the void."

With one hand shadowing his face he rose from the earth, mute and sorrowful; and tears, the first that had ever yet dimmed immortal eyes, oozed out from between the unstained whiteness of his fingers, and fell like a shower upon the ground. He looked upon the earth, and stood ankle-deep in the blue flowers of the Forget-me-not — they had sprung from the angel's tears; and high in the air he heard a floating, unembodied voice, sweeter than that music which had cheered his lonely watch, when he kept guard beside the battlements of heaven, while the helmed cherubims flew forth to wage war against the fallen angels. It was the voice of her for whose love he had sacrificed heaven: and, kneeling amid the blue flowers, with clasped hands, motionless as a statue, the low, aërial music shaped itself into words, as it fell upon his ear; and he held his breath with awe, for he knew that it was now an immortal voice which said,—

By the wold and by the wildwood,
By lonely mere, and water'd lea,
Haunts of age, and sportive childhood,
I am doomed to follow thee:
By the torrent it was utter'd,
'Mid the flowers that round it blow,
And upon the breeze was mutter'd
The sad sentence of our woe—
And each bud and bell that's hollow,
Bade thee lead where I must follow.

Till the flowers thy feet surrounding
Shall be planted everywhere,
No shaded stream but what they're found in,
Throughout the summers of each year:

And in remembrance of our sorrow,
   Many a maid shall seek that spot
In twilight glooms,—and when the morrow
   Gilds the sweet Forget-me-not—
Where the river murmurs hollow,
Lovers ages hence shall follow.

And where the forest brook runs brawling,—
   Here in sunshine, there in shade,
Lovers shall be oft heard calling,
   While they traverse glen and glade:
As they search each woodland spot,
   Hazelled dell and briery brake,
For the blue Forget-me-not,
   Which they'll cherish for our sake—
And up to Heaven's high arching hollow,
Many a sigh our loves shall follow.

And in the flower they shall see blended,
   The golden star that emblems thee,
Rimmed with the blue thy wings descended—
   The heaven thou'st lost, for love of me:
Without repining, or complaining,
   Must thy weary task be done,
If thou hast hopes of e'er regaining
   Those lost realms beyond the sun—
For the voice said, low and hollow,
" Where he goeth thou shalt follow."

Every one who has wandered by the meadow-streams and woodland brooks of pastoral England has gathered the blue Forget-me-not, one of the most beautiful of our water-loving flowers; looking, where a bed of it is growing together, as if the blue of heaven had dropped down, and blended with the green tint of the earth. Nor is its azure-eyed sister of the meadow (the *Mysotis arvensis*) less fair: but its legend has yet to be written, and the gentle spirit portrayed who first planted it in the fields of Waterloo above the graves of England's fallen heroes.

The Myrtle had its birth in the sunny clime of the East, and first grew amid those gardens where the dark-eyed daughters of the sun, as they floated through the mazy circles of the dreamy dance, shook out their silken ringlets to the dallying wind. In many a peaceful valley which nestles down between the mountain-passes is it found, with its beautiful white blossoms blowing amid the untrodden solitudes, and filling the air with fragrance for miles around. The fair maidens of Judea bore it in their processions, and twined its scented branches into green arbours at their solemn festivals. And among the ancient traditions of the Arabs it is recorded, that Adam bore in his hand a sprig of Myrtle when he was driven from the garden of Paradise,—it might be from the very bower where he first breathed his love into the ear of Eve.

In spring the green woods of merry England are covered with the flowers of the Anemone. Turn the eye whichever way you will, there it greets you like "a pleasant thought:" it forms a bed of flowers around the foot of the mighty oak, and below the tangling brambles, which you may peep between, but cannot pass,—there, also, are its pearly blossoms bending. The Greeks named it the Flower of the Wind, and so plentiful is it in our own country that we might fancy the breeze had blown it everywhere. The gaudy Anemone of the garden, the emblem of Forsaken Love, is known to all; but our favourites are the uncultivated offspring of the windy woods, which come long before the broad green leaves hang overhead to shelter them.

The Laurustinus is a beautiful evergreen, bearing white flowers; which, before they become opened, have all the richness of the Rose about the colour of the buds. Why so hardy a plant was selected for the image of Neglected Love we know not, unless it be that Love dies a hard death, and is difficult to destroy. Milton has found a much more poetical image in

"The ratho Primrose that forsaken dies,"

than in the Anemone; and for the sake of the Bard

of Paradise, the Primrose should have been held inviolable to Forsaken or Neglected Love. It is a more poetical flower than either of the above, and although we have followed our predecessors in nothing but their ill-chosen names, yet our emblem of Forsaken Love is the Primrose, so christened by Milton at his own Immortal Font.

FORGET-ME-NOT.

Forget thee, love? — no, not whilst heaven
  Spans its starred vault across the sky;
Oh, may I never be forgiven,
  If e'er I cause that heart a sigh!
Sooner shall the Forget-me-not
  Shun the fringed brook by which it grows,
And pine for some sequestered spot,
  Where not a silver ripple flows.
By the blue heaven that bends above me,
Dearly and fondly do I love thee!

They fabled not in days of old
  That Love neglected soon will perish,—
Throughout all time the truth doth hold
  That what we love we ever cherish.

For when the Sun neglects the Flower,
  And the sweet pearly dews forsake it,
It hangs its head, and from that hour
  Prays only unto Death to take it.
So may I droop, by all above me,
If once this heart doth cease to love thee!

The Turtle-Dove that 's lost its mate,
  Hides in some gloomy greenwood shade,
And there alone mourns o'er its fate,
  With plumes for ever disarrayed:
Alone! alone! it there sits cooing:—
  Deem'st thou, my love, what it doth seek?
'Tis Death the mournful bird is wooing,
  In murmurs through its plaintive beak.
So will I mourn, by all above me,
If in this world I cease to love thee!

THE VIOLET OF THE VALLEY.

YOUR MODESTY AND AMIABILITY HAVE CAUSED ME TO CONFESS MY LOVE.

EMBLEMS.

MODESTY—*BLUE VIOLET:* AMIABILITY—*WHITE JASMINE:*
CONFESSION OF LOVE—*MOSS-ROSE:*
PURE LOVE—*PINK.*

"Violets dim,
But sweeter than the lids of Juno's eyes,
Or Cytherea's breath."—SHAKSPEARE.

IN one of those secluded valleys, the beauty of which astonishes the traveller as he comes upon it unaware, stood a neat-looking, lowly-thatched cottage, like a hidden nest embosomed amid the green tranquillity of the hills. A winding footpath threaded its way towards the breezy summit,—here running

along the narrow level of a ledge, there making a graceful bend round the bole of some majestic tree, and farther on climbing upward, with a steep, breathless ascent, until the level brow of the hill was gained. Then, far as the eye could wander, it commanded a view, over a vast outstretched landscape, diversified with spires, and plains, and woods, intercepted every way with a broad clear river, that went rolling and bending along, until it dwindled into a mere thread of silver, as it was lost in the distance. On the brow of this beautiful hill a plain rustic seat had been erected by the inhabitants of the cottage in the valley; and as there was no thoroughfare beyond what was traversed by the neighbouring villagers, who came morning and evening to milk the cows, which were heard lowing amongst the hilly fields, the summit, like the valley it overlooked, was seldom trodden by the foot of a stranger. And often on a summer's evening, when the labour of the day was over, might the form of a lovely maiden be seen leaving that cottage, and climbing the steep ascent of the hill, carrying either a little work-basket on her arm, or a book in her hand, and every now and then pausing to look over the landscape, as she threaded her way to the rustic seat. Sometimes she sent forth her voice in gushing music, which was prolonged and reverberated through the dale, as if the echoes of the valley were her companions, and their only delight were to call to and answer each other. She sang from the very overjoyousness of her heart, like a bird, perched amid a cluster of milk-white blossoms, that takes a delight in telling the trees, and flowers, and sunshine, which hang around it, how great is the pleasure that fills its little heart, and how happy it is in the companionship of such sweet scenery: and should the form of a stranger appear, the golden chain of her melody was snapped asunder in an instant, and, like a bird, she would dart down to her little thatched nest in the valley below. Her modesty, and the sweetness of her voice, had obtained for her, amidst the neighbouring villagers, the name of The Violet of the Valley.

Those who know not the bliss which springs from contentment, might marvel how one so beautiful could rest satisfied by burying herself in such seclusion. They might as well have asked the Violet why it was so happy in the solitude which surrounded it, why it concealed its beauty amid the green leaves by which it was overhung, and scattered its sweetness upon "the desert air;" and the Violet might have replied, that although the air which blew around it was deserted, yet many a breeze would carry its sweetness afar off, perfuming unseen and distant places that were not solitary. Although her beauty had not gladdened the gaze of many beholders, still her voice on a calm summer's evening had fallen with a peaceful hush on many a gentle heart, coming upon the ear

> "Like the sweet south,
> That breathes upon a bank of Violets,
> Stealing and giving odour:"

for hers were sweet and rustic strains,—unstudied melodies, that stole in and out of the heart: they were "old and plain," such as

> "The spinsters and the knitters, in the sun,
> And the free maids that weave their thread with bone,
> Do use to chant: for they were silly truth,
> And dallied with the innocence of love
> Like th' olden age."

They were such as Barbara was wont to chant when she went singing about the house before she "hung her head aside," and all for love; for within that innocent heart Love had not yet "lighted his golden torch, and waved his purple wings." The temple and the shrine were there, but within that holy place no worshipper had as yet knelt down—no incense was offered up excepting from the flowers, those bowing adorers of that tranquil valley. The anthems that echoed there were the songs of the wild birds, and the prayer breathed forth was the adoration of Nature, ministering in her own holy temple. If Love was there, it sat like a child playing in its innocence upon its own hearth, admiring the starry Jasmine which threw its green curtaining over the casement, or looking fondly at the Moss-rose which peeped in timidly at the latticed doorway. There was an unstudied grace in her attitude which the eye of the sculptor hath not yet caught,—a finish about the turning of the head and the rounding of the shoulders, to which marble hath not yet lent its enduring immortality ; while in the large blue heaven of her downcast eyes, Modesty ever seemed to sit enthroned. In her casual visits to the distant market-town, men turned their heads in wonderment, and even women marvelled from whence such a being of life and beauty had sprung ; for wherever she moved, she seemed to throw across the pavement a glad streak as if of sunshine. The astonished stranger made his inquiries in vain,—all he could gather was, that she was called the Violet of the Valley, but where she dwelt there were few that knew. And many an eye ere it closed in sleep pictured that form moving before it, until slumber settled down, and in dreams they were carried away to far-off dells and dingles; to valleys where the nightingale made music all summer long: and they thought of Eve before she fell, and believed that somewhere in the earth there still existed an unvisited Paradise. They pictured a rustic home which the amiable Jasmine overhung, without knowing that with such her own was garlanded. They conjured up a porch twined over with Moss-roses, unconscious that the threshold over which her beauty passed was wreathed with the same queenly flowers. In their sleep they sighed over perfumed beds of Pinks, not knowing that her own garden was covered with them ; and they built up an imaginary abode for Love to dwell in, before the winged god had either alighted upon, or visited the spot. Many a sigh was sent over the hills which overlooked that little cottage, and many a prayer wafted towards the happy valley in which she dwelt; but the bees murmured round her home, the butterflies sat swinging upon her flowers, morning and evening the birds swelled their anthems upon the breeze, and all night long the brook went singing to itself beneath her window, and, excepting an affection for all those sweet sights and sounds, and a heart at peace with all mankind, she was as yet untouched by Love.

But Love at length came, timid as he ever cometh: concealing himself at first behind the trees, or screened by the surrounding bushes, as if all he coveted was to listen to the music of her voice. When he appeared, she vanished; when he retreated, she was again in her accustomed place. It was as if the sunshine was sporting with the beautiful shadow, and both vanished at the same moment of time,—as if Love and Modesty were ashamed of accosting each other, though they were ever sighing when alone to be made one. Until one day Love, emboldened, left a posy upon her favourite rural seat, hiding himself while he watched the Violet of the Valley untwining her sister flowers. As she held them in her hand the Moss-rose fell against her bosom, and she felt a strange fluttering from within, which told her that Love was folding his wings, and taking possession of his new abode. While from her heaving heart arose this confession, her cheek became blanched until it was paler than the blossoms of the Jasmine; then over all arose a flushing warmth, the pearly pinkness of blushing love, mantling her cheek, and making it more beautiful than the most delicate crimson with which the Moss-rose was dyed :—and from that day Love and Modesty dwelt together, their abode embowered about with Jasmine, and trailing Roses, and Violets, sweet as the perfumes of Paradise.

Love could not have found a happier nor a more peaceful home. The very spot in which they dwelt was a land of perfect poetry, and within it her simple wishes were bounded; for she knew no more about what the world calls rank, and splendour, and fashion, than the modest Violet, after which she was named, does of the flowers that are forced into bloom and beauty within the unnatural atmosphere of a hothouse. "The heart," says an old writer, "envieth not that which it hath never known, neither doth the eye covet what it hath never seen, and from this very ignorance cometh much happiness." Spring came, and poured her opening buds into the valley, and let loose her feathered songsters amongst the trees. Summer followed, and, with sunny fingers, opened the flowers, giving freedom to a thousand imprisoned perfumes. Then came Autumn, with his wheaten sheaf and ruddy fruitage,—and when all these were gone, she had still Love left for her companion throughout the dark Winter; and, knowing that the bright seasons would soon return again, there was nothing in the world that she coveted.

Every one can remember some bank on which the Violet blows—some green lane or pleasant foot-path in which they have been stopped in spring by its fragrance. "Sweet Violets" is one of the earliest cries which greet the ear in spring, telling us that they have come again, like beautiful children, heralding in the approach of summer; they bring joyous tidings of brighter days, and the return of singing birds, and the whispers of long leaves, and the memory of pleasant walks, reminding us that Nature has awoke from her slumber, and is shaking open the unblown buds, whieh have gathered around her during her long winter's sleep. Dear was this modest and beautiful flower to the hearts of our elder poets, and from its sweetness, buried amid the broad green leaves, they drew forth many an exquisite image, and in it found the emblems of hidden Virtue, and neglected Modesty, and unchanging Love.

Stepping further into Summer, comes the star-white Jasmine,—that sweet perfumer of the night, whieh only throws out its full fragranee when its sister stars are keeping watch in the sky; as if, when the song of the nightingale no longer cheered the darkness, it sent forth its silent aroma upon the listening air. Many a happy home does it garland, and peeps in at many a forbidden lattiee, where Love and Beauty repose. Little did the proud eourtiers and stately dames of Queen Elizabeth's day dream that this sweet-scented ereeper (a sprig of which seemed to make the haughty, haughtier still) would one day become so common as to eluster around, and embower, thousands of humble English cottages,—a degradation which, could they but have witnessed, would almost have made every plait of their starehed ruffs bristle up, like "quills upon the fretful porcupine." Beautiful are its long, drooping, dark-green shoots, trailing around the trellis-work of a doorway, like a green curtain embroidered with silver flowers; while here and there the queenly Moss-rose, creeping in and out like the threads of a fanciful tapestry, shows its crimson face amid the embowered green, —a beautiful lady peeping through a leaf-clad casement.

But of all the odours that ever floated from the spicy shores of "Araby the Blest," there are few to excel the sweet fragrance of our scented Pinks; over which, when the wind blows, the gale seems to come laden as if with perfume from a bed of spices. Beautiful are they in their wild state, waving on the ruined walls of some ancient fortress, and drooping peacefully over those mouldering battlements, behind which the warder once paced, and the crossbowman took his deadly aim,—there it still hangs, throwing its sweetness over the roofless walls of the banquet-hall, as if to show how frail and fleeting was the beauty which once proudly trod those crumbling floors.

Alas! the breathing beauties have departed, and only the flowers are now remaining behind. They are gone who loved to see themselves wreathed around with blossoms, and thought their loveliness still lovelier when adorned with Summer's opening buds; for amid all the rich stores which Imagination suggested, they could find no tints that excelled, no shapes that surpassed, no fragrance that outsweetened, the breath of the flowers. From the deep purple which the haughty emperors wore, to the shaded and delicate colours which mingled in the varied costume of the crowned Queen,—when the loom had exhausted its richness, and the unsunned mine brought to light the splendour of its treasures, they were still eclipsed by the matchless attire of the flowers; for "Solomon in all his glory was not arrayed like one of these."

FLOWERS OF LOVE.

WITH grey head bent upon the ground,
 While wandering through a Saxon vale,
A Pilgrim first the Vi'let found,
 Flinging its fragrance on the gale,
As he towards the holy shrine
 Journey'd along with wearied feet:—
He smiled to think the saint divine
 Should him with such sweet odours meet.

A Lover on the Indian sea,
 Sighing for her left far behind,
Inhaled the scented Jasmine-tree,
 As it perfumed the evening wind:

Shoreward he steer'd at dawn of day,
  And saw the coast all round embower'd,
And brought a starry sprig away,
  For her by whose green cot it flower'd.

And oft when from that scorching shore,
  In after-days, those odours came,
He pictured his green cottage door,
  The shady porch, and window-frame,
Far, far away across the foam:
  The very Jasmine-flower that crept
Round the thatch'd roof about his home,
  Where she he loved still safely slept.

With raven-ringlets blown apart,
  And trembling like a startled dove,
A lovely girl press'd to her heart
  A Moss-rose, to appease its love.
But all in vain, it still kept beating,—
  And so she said, "'Tis all in vain!
Oh, this love, 'tis past defeating,—
  What can I do but love again?"

OLD SAXON FLOWERS.

YOUR HUMILITY, AND CONSTANCY, AND PURITY OF HEART, CLAIM MY AFFECTIONATE REMEMBRANCE.

EMBLEMS.

HUMILITY—*BROOM:* CONSTANCY—*CANTERBURY BELL:* PURITY OF HEART—*WHITE WATER-LILY:* AFFECTIONATE REMEMBRANCE—*ROSEMARY.*

Oft musing by the greenwood side,
'Mid Blue-bells deep, and golden Broom,
Time's ancient gateway open wide,
And far adown the gathering gloom,
On many a mouldering Saxon tomb,
The oldest flowers of England bloom.

BEAUTIFUL art thou, O Broom! waving in all thy rich array of green and gold, on the breezy bosom of the bee-haunted heath. The sleeping sunshine, and the silver-footed showers, the clouds that for ever play about the face of Heaven, the homeless winds, and the crystal-globed dews, that settle upon thy blossoms like sleep on the veined

eyelids of an infant, are ever beating above and around thee, as if to tell that they rejoice in thy companionship, and that, although a thousand years have strided by with silent steps, Time hath not abated an atom of their love. Who can tell the thoughts of Saxon Alfred when, wandering alone crownless and sceptreless, he stretched himself on the lonely moor beneath the shadow of thy golden blossoms, sighing for the fair queen he had left far behind? When he bowed his kingly head, and, musing on thy beauty, buried in a solitary wild, thought how even regal dignity would be enhanced by Humility, and that, although thou didst grow there unmarked and unpruned, not a more princely flower waved in his own English garden. And thus musing he might pluck the Blue-bell that nodded beside thee, and see imaged in the humble and beautiful flower, an emblem of Constancy,—might mark how ye still grew together side by side, how the yellow Broom sheltered the azure Bell which bloomed beneath it from storm and wind, and how, when the sunshine streamed out, the constant flower opened its blue eyes and looked upward, and thus they became enamoured of each other. That his thoughtful eye glanced over the silent waters of the lonely mere, where the White Water-lily sat, like a crowned queen upon a green throne of rounded leaves, receiving homage from a thousand ripples, which were ever bowing down and kissing the pearly whiteness of her feet. How the snowy petals of this pale princess of the waters might recall the Purity of Heart of her he loved, how he might trace the outline of her beautiful brow in the golden crown of the flower, see in the silver-skirted ripples the moving forms of her attendants, and, catching another glimpse of the yellow Broom, and the rounded Blue-bell, conjure up the Humility and Constancy, and Purity of his own queen; and, taking heart, strike some sad, sweet note on the silent harp, which had hitherto lain neglected beside him, and see rising before him a thousand homes, which no misbelieving Dane had ravished, and a kingdom freed from the desolating hand of the invader. How, on a future day, some proud Plantagenet might have heard the legend from the sweet lips of the fair Saxon he had espoused, and he might mount the humble Broom in his haughty helmet, his cheek blanching while he gazed over the possessions he had gained by plunder and power, as he thought how, in former days, the recovery of a kingdom had been planned, and won back, by a brave and houseless king; whose throne was then a solitary heath, canopied by a blue and bounded sky, and his attendants only the surrounding flowers.

Who can tell what sad feelings hung about the

heart of the fair Saxon princess Ethelberga when, standing in the twilight, on the broom-covered steep hill-side, she saw from the distance the fires kindled by the hands of the desolating Dane, and beheld the flames which devoured the home of her childhood reddening in the evening sky? It might be that whilst she found a couch amongst the waving gold of the wild, surrounded by her houseless attendants, and pillowed her beautiful head upon the Broom, she selected it as the emblem of Humility. And when she saw the waving Blue-bells spring up on the very spot where the stormy sea-kings had encamped—where the tide of battle had raged, and swollen, and subsided, leaving no other trace of its course than the silent ridges which had heaped up over the dead; she selected the blue-cupped flower as the true image of Constancy; which, though crushed, and bruised, and buried, forsaketh not the chosen spot where its beauty first bloomed. That when she sat mournful beside the moorland mere, wearied through carrying water to quench the thirst of the brave Saxons, who had been wounded in battle, she saw the pale Water-lilies sleeping upon their dark-green velvet leaves, spotless as the clear element upon which they floated, and leaving no vestige of the gross earth from which they sprung; and she thought how the heart of a woman, ennobled by virtuous deeds, might become so purified, that if looked into by the eye of an angel, he could not discover within, either blot or blemish, nor aught that varied from his own divinity, but the fond humanity of love. Musing, she might conjure up some grey old Saxon abbey, nestling amid the silence of a green, sequestered valley, with its quiet graves, around which the Rosemary grew, hallowed the more in its remembrance, through having been brought by holy men across the pathless sea; and she might think that even as that plant put forth its flowers in the dead midnight of winter, so through the deep clouds which hung over and darkened her native land, the morning of peace might yet break, and see many a battle-field again overgrown with flowers.

It was in those days that Love and Constancy set out together to visit the world, and look for the abode of Happiness: for there were rumours abroad that she had concealed herself somewhere in the earth, and they were fearful that Happiness had long pined for their society, and grown weary in waiting for their coming. Humility went with them; and Affectionate Remembrance, a lovely maiden, who sighed as often as she smiled, was also their attendant. Many a time would she have sunk by the way, had not Love and Constancy consoled her; while Humility led her by the hand and whispered words of hope, whenever she felt low and desponding. "I cannot help it," said Remembrance; "but when I look into the past I see more of pain than pleasure; and as for the future, it is so chequered with hopes and fears that whilst 'I doat I doubt;' and there ever seems some sorrow overhanging and ready to settle down upon what I love." "Take heart," said Constancy, "all will yet be well; even Love is sometimes fretful, and it is only by leaning upon him, and looking into his face, that I can comfort him; for he seems as if he sometimes had forgotten that I was still at his side."

Humility, and Constancy, and Purity of Heart, are the very divinities of Love, and among the holiest images which we enshrine in the innermost temple of the soul. Humility, like a lowly and beautiful maiden, ever walketh abroad with downcast and modest glance, her hands folded meekly, and her free thoughts wandering like graceful handmaids through the charmed chambers of the mind; unfettered by the painful panoply of pride, and unimpeded by the watchful sentries who ever keep jealous guard around the slave of ambition. On her cheek the healthy beams of morning beat, and the dews of dawning are the pearly gems which diadem her brow: there is a grace in the unstudied flow of her drapery which the artists of old seized upon, when they called forth from the canvas forms which embodied the divinity of woman. They drew the adoration of the angels from her looks, and the great masters flew to her expressive features; then they shadowed forth the Virgin-mother bending over her Holy Child; for there is no love without humility, no true affection unless it see in the object of its worship a divinity towards which it tremblingly aspires.

"Constancy," says the poet, "liveth in realms above: but kind Pity, who had long looked down with tender eyes, and beheld how cheerless and restless the wandering heart was, even though it fondly loved, sent her down upon the earth as a comforter, and she took up her abode within the blue-belled flowers of the wild. She gathered together all the floating affections of true hearts, and formed for them many a sweet habitation, which they had sighed for in vain, to dwell in. She erected for them a new and pleasant home in the heart,—she assembled round them a thousand household virtues,—and what the eye had before sought for abroad in vain, it found within; it became the resting-place of Love, and there alone was true beauty to be found. Man no longer sighed for the Paradise he had lost, for Constancy led him by the hand and brought him back; and he sat enthroned amid a lovelier Eden in the beating heart of woman.

Abroad he saw her image everywhere reflected.

The Water-lily sleeping on the lake mirrored back the purity in which he now dwelt; all around beside her might move, but Constancy had anchored her true roots within the heart,—an hundred contending waves might watch over the spotless snow of her blossoms, but she still rose triumphant, whiter and purer from the contest; for the washing of every ripple but laid bare some hidden virtue, and from every assault she won back some lost affection.

And when Love and Constancy set out to wander hand in hand through the world, with Humility and Affectionate Remembrance for their attendants, within was found that Purity of Heart which ever ensureth devoted attachment; it was then that they made a happy home wherever they alighted, and carried with them a sweet sunshine, which threw its brightness around the shadiest places. In old primeval forests they sometimes dwelt, far away from the fever and the fret of busy cities,—they found a shelter beneath the yellow Broom, and a couch amid the azure Bells of flowers. Where huge sandy deserts stretched for miles away they pitched their tent, and in the deep caverns of majestic mountains Love and Constancy took up their abode. They tended their cattle together on vast plains, and followed Summer over many a high hill and outstretched valley; sojourning together in rude huts, whose branched walls and leafy roofs bore the first rough tracings of the primitive home of man. The feudal castle raised its grim and grated portcullis to receive them, and the iron archers threw down their tight-strung bows to welcome their approach. They slept together in sheds where the hardy serf struggled against wrong, and laid many a night on the bleak hill-side, where the lonely shepherd tended his flock. They accompanied many brave hearts that went forth reluctantly to wage war against the invaders of their country, and as they conversed together they beguiled the listless cheerlessness of the way. Wherever they went old age coveted no other companionship, nor did they leave a grey head to sink down in sorrow to the grave. They gave to poverty content, to affliction resignation, and into the sad heart of pity they breathed hope.

It was then that mankind began to find deep matter for meditation in the flowers; that they no longer looked upon the blossoms as the mere harbingers of the seasons, and beautiful ornamenters of the fields, but discovered that they were lettered over with the language of Love,—that Beauty bloomed where no human eye perceived it, in sequestered nooks and untrodden wilds, and Nature needed not the presence of man, to either look upon or praise her works. They believed that hidden spirits dwelt among the flowers of the woods, and that not a Bell waved in the solitudes of the pathless dell, but what had its own fair minister, for they were the first to discover

> "That there are more things in heaven and earth
> Than are dreamt of in our philosophy."

That the " airy tongues which syllable men's names," sounding on lonely moors, and amid the silence of solemn forests, are invisible spirits, which linger about the earth, until the human heart becomes purified by Love — and a fitting habitation for them to dwell in. That as there is nothing in the ocean but what hath its representative on land, so is there no virtue upon earth but what is found in a purer form in heaven,—that Divine Love sends down its essence like a stream of light, and that all which prevents it from becoming in man what it is in the angels, is the perishable mortality in which we are clothed.

The Descent of Spring was ever beautiful, from the first moment that she planted her white feet upon the daisied green of April, to when she stretched herself upon the couch of flowers, which had sprung up of their own accord that she might recline upon their sweetness. For her the leaves grow longer every day, that under their shade she may find shelter when the silver-footed showers descend. Her eyes are ever blue as her own April skies; her cheeks dyed with the delicate crimson of the apple-blossoms; her white and blue-veined neck beautiful as a bed of lilies-of-the-valley, intersected with trailing violets; while her silken air streams out like the graceful acacias, that throw their gold and green upon the breeze. Around her brow is twined a wreath of May-blossoms—pearly buds, but yet unblown. High above her head the skylark soars, while the linnet warbles in the brake, and from every tree and bush an hundred choristers raise their voices in the great concert which they hold to welcome her. The sunbeams that dance about the primrose-coloured sky—the insects that hum and wanton in the air, the flowers that day by day rise higher above the bladed grass, and the bursting buds that grow bolder as they venture out further from the hedgerows to peep at her beauty, all proclaim with what delight the return of Spring is ever hailed.

We know not what visions the great poets may have seen in the earlier ages, when they described Spring as a beautiful maiden descending from heaven, and scattering flowers upon the earth. They may have caught glimpses of the immortal goddess as she cleaved her way through the sky, and hung poised for a moment upon the skirt of some silver cloud. In the blue and deepening twilight, as they went musing by the side of some hoary forest, they may have seen, through the evening shadows, eyes peering amid the dim foliage, as bright as the stars which hang in the bending arch of heaven: for we know not what forms visit the folded flowers, as they bow their heads and seem to sleep through the still night; nor can we tell what the leaves say to one another when they whisper together, or what wisdom is uttered by "those green-robed senators of mighty woods." Titania and her fairy train may yet haunt many a bank

> "Whereon the wild thyme blows,
> Where ox-lips and the nodding violet grows;
> Quite o'ercanopied with lush woodbine,
> With sweet musk-roses and with eglantine."

The White Water-lily is the Queen of the Waves, and reigns sole sovereign over the streams; and it was a species of Water-lily which the old Egyptians and ancient Indians worshipped—the most beautiful object that was held sacred in their superstitious creed—and one which we cannot look upon even now without feeling a delight mingled with reverence. No flower looks more lovely than this "Lady of the Lake," resting her crowned head on a green throne of velvet, and looking down into the depths of her own sky-reflecting realms, watching the dance, as her attendant water-nymphs keep time to the rocking of the ripples, and the dreamy swaying of the trailing water-stems. Whether or not this Queen of the Waters retires to her own crystal dominions after sunset, and sleeps in her silver palace beneath the ripples, seems to be a matter of doubt amongst botanists. To an old angler like myself, who has lost many a hook, and had his lines entangled, amongst their stems after they had sunk below the waters, there can be no doubt at all; but whether this might be the case in very shallow streams, or "made ponds," is another matter; my experience is confined to ancient delfts and old out-of-the-way meres and places, that yet retain their ancient Saxon names, where the true English Water-lilies still grow. The bard of Erin says,—

"Those virgin lilies all the night
Bathing their beauties in the lake,
That they may rise more fresh and bright,
When their beloved sun 's awake."

The "Bonny Broom" is familiar to every lover of the country, and cannot be mistaken for the gorse or furze, even in the dark; for, although their flowers are very similar, there is a difference in the latter, which is soon "felt." The Broom is one of England's oldest flowers, and was as familiar to the eye of the ancient Briton as it is to our own; neither has its name undergone any change, for Alfred the Great called it the Broom, as we do now. I have chosen to carry it farther back than the days of the Plantagenets, for the origin of its emblem, as there is but little of Humility about their haughty race, whatever there may be in their name.

Blue-belled flowers, known by a hundred various names in different parts of England, and all belonging to the genus *Campanula*, are as familiar as the Daisy to every one who has rambled about the country — from the campion (the giant) to the creeping, and every variety of bell-shaped flower that belongs to the order. But of all the Blue-bells, my favourite is the little wild Hare-bell, which still gets as near into London as it can for the smoke, and may be found no farther off than Dulwich and Norwood, growing by the dusty roadside, under the shade of hedges, by dry ditches, and in spots where scarcely any other flowers are to be found it may be seen nodding its beautiful blue head, when nearly all the blossoms of summer have faded. There, together with the heather, it still blows, in spite of railways and land-surveyors, and will do until the foundations for new houses have uprooted it from its native spot; until human habitations are reared, and household hearths blaze above the place where it has for ages shaken its beautiful blue-bells to the breeze. That botanist displayed some taste who first selected these bell-shaped flowers as the emblem of Constancy, for "true blue" is one of the few colours about which Britons boast; they are truly English flowers —

"Sweet daughters of the earth and sky."

The Rosemary is so often mentioned by our early writers, both in prose, poetry, and our oldest dramas, that a long article, possessing great interest to such as love old-fashioned things, might be written upon it. The Rosemary was used both at their feasts and their funerals,—the christening-cup was stirred with it, and it was worn at their marriage ceremonies. Shakspeare has chosen it for the emblem of Remembrance, and who would attempt to change the meaning of a flower which his genius has hallowed, or disturb a leaf over which he has breathed his holy "superstition?"—in memory of him we use the latter word in all reverence. A few years ago it was customary in many parts of England to plant slips of Rosemary over the dead, nor has the practice yet fallen altogether into disuse,—rural cemeteries will revive these ancient customs. But I have entered rather lengthily into this subject in my "Pictures of Country Life," under the article headed "Rural Cemeteries," so have good reason for not going again over the same ground. Shakspeare, who never even gathered an image from a flower, or selected it as an emblem, without first examining its appropriate nature, chose the Rosemary as the representative of Remembrance, for it flowers in winter. How beautiful and poetical is this allusion! When all around beside is withered and decayed, when the

"Wind and rain beat dark December,"

and the gaudy Summer is dead and buried, with all her wreathed flowers; it was then that from the only one which came to look upon and cheer man by its presence, he chose the Rosemary, and said—

"That's for Remembrance;
I pray you, love, remember."

OLD SAXON FLOWERS.

The Lily on the water sleeping,
Enwreath'd with pearl, and boss'd with gold,
An emblem is, my love, of thee:
But when she like a nymph is peeping,

To watch her sister-buds unfold,
White-shoulder'd, on the flowery Lea,
Gazing about in sweet amazement,
Thy image, from the vine-clad casement,
Seems looking out, my love, on me.

No marvel that my heart became
Attached to thee—in all around me
I saw the likeness of thy face;
Within the Broom I spelt thy name,
In every Blue-bell'd flower I found thee,
In all fair things I could thee trace;
No bud, nor bell, the stem adorning,
Hung with the trembling gems of morning,
The dew,—but call'd up thy embrace.

In thee I found a new delight,—
Alone my heart was ever sighing,
And pining for another heart;
Like flowers that bow beneath the night,
The very fragrance in them dying,
So did I droop from thee apart;
Till on me broke thy beauteous splendour,—
Thine eyes that looked—oh, heaven! how tender:
I cannot tell thee what thou art.

Thou'rt like the Water-lily pure,
That grows where rippling waters rumble.

Constant as are the flowers of blue,
That every stormy change endure;
And, like the Broom, though ever Humble,
They die, but never change their hue:
The Rosemary, that in December
Still says, "I pray you, love, remember:"
Through storms and snow remaining true.

HOW THE ROSE BECAME RED.

YOUR PREFERENCE WOULD BRING ME CONSOLATION; YOUR LOVE A RETURN OF HAPPINESS.

EMBLEMS.

PREFERENCE—*APPLE-BLOSSOM:* CONSOLATION—*POPPY:* LOVE—*ROSE:* RETURN OF HAPPINESS—*VIOLET OF THE VALLEY.*

"Sometimes she shakes her head, and then his hand,
Now gazeth she on him, now on the ground:
Sometimes her arms enfold him like a band;
She would:—he will not in her arms be bound;
And when from thence he struggles to be gone,
She locks her fingers (*round him*) one in one."

SHAKSPEARE'S *Venus and Adonis.*

IT was drawing towards the decline of a beautiful summer day, when the red, round sun was bending down a deep, blue, unclouded sky, to where a vast range of mountains stretched, summit upon summit, and in the far distance again arose, pile upon pile,

until high over all towered the god-haunted height of cloud-capt Olympus, rising with its clouded head, like another world, on the uttermost rim of the horizon. At the foot of this immense world of untrodden mountains opened out a wide, immeasurable forest, stretching far away, league beyond league, with its unpeopled ocean of trees, which were bounded somewhere by another range of unknown mountains, that again overlooked a vast, silent, and unexplored world. On the edge of this pathless desert of trees, and nearest the foot of Olympus, sat the Queen of Beauty and of Love; with her golden tresses unbound, and her matchless countenance buried within the palms of her milk-white hands, while sobbing as if her fond, immortal heart, would break. Beside her was laid the dead body of Adonis, his face half hidden beneath the floating fall of her hair, as she bent over him and wept. Beyond them lay the stiffened bulk of the grim and grisly boar, his hideous jaws flecked with blood and foam, and his terrible tusks glittering like the heads of pointed spears, as they stood out sharp and white in the unclouded sunset. Not an immortal comforter was by: for the far-seeing eye of Jove was fixed listlessly upon the golden nectar-cup, as it passed from hand to hand, along the rounded circle of the Gods, whilst they were recounting the deeds of other days, when they waged war against the Titans. Even the chariot of Venus stood unyoked at the foot of the mount; the silken traces lay loosely thrown together upon the ground, and the white doves were idly hovering round in the air; for the weeping goddess was so overwhelmed with sorrow, that she had forgotten to waft her lightning-winged whisper to the Mount of Olympus; nor had they received any summons from the charioteer Love, who with folded wings lay sleeping upon a bed of roses, with his bow and arrows by his side.

In the glade of this vast forest of the old primeval world—whose echoes had never been startled by the blows of a descending axe, nor a branch rent from their majestic boles, saving by the dreaded bolts of the Thunderer, or some earth-shaking storm, which, in his anger, he had blown abroad,—the Goddess of Beauty still continued to sit, as if unconscious of the savage solitude which surrounded her; nor did she notice the back-kneed Satyrs, that peered upon her unrobed loveliness with burning eyes, from many a shadowy recess in the thick-leaved underwood. Upon the trunks of the mighty and storm-tortured trees, the sunset here and there flashed down in rays of molten gold, making their gnarled and twisted stems look as if they had just issued red-hot from the jaws of some cavern-like furnace, whose glare the fancy might still trace in a blackened avenue of trees, up which the red ranks of the consuming lightning had ages agone marched. Every way, where the lengthened shadows of evening began to fall in deeper masses, the forest assumed a more savage look, which was heightened by the noise of some deadly-tusked boar as he went snorting and thundering through the thicket; the growl of the tiger was also heard at intervals, as he retreated farther into the deepening darkness of the dingles, mistaking the blaze of sunset for some devouring fire. But the eyes of Venus saw only the pale face of her lover,—she felt only his chilly and stiffened hand sink colder and deeper into the warm heart on which she pressed it, and over which her tears fell, slower or faster, just as the mournful gusts of her sorrow arose or subsided, and sent the blinding rain from the blue-veined lids that overhung her clouded eyes; for never had her immortal heart before been swollen by such an overflowing torrent of grief. But the warmth of her kisses, which would almost have awakened life in a statue of marble, fell upon lips now cold as a wintry grave; and her sighs, which came sweeter than the morning air when it first arises from its sleep amongst the roses, stirred not one of the clotted ringlets which softened into the yielding whiteness of her heavenly bosom,—

"She looked upon his lips, and they are pale;
She took him by the hand, and that was cold;
She whispered in his ears a heavy tale,
As if they heard the woeful words she told."

She would have given her immortality but to have heard those lips murmur and complain, as they had done a few hours before—to have seen those eyes again burning with disdain as they flashed back indignantly the warm advances of her love. She pictured him as he had that very morning stood, in all the pride of youthful manliness and beauty, when he looked down, blushing and abashed, as he held his boar-spear in his hand, when she threw the studded bridle over her own rounded and naked arm, and the proud courser pricked up his ears with delight, and shook his braided mane, while his long tail streamed out like a banner, and his proud eye dilated, and his broad nostrils expanded, as he went trampling haughtily on, proud to be led by the Queen of Beauty and of Love. She pictured the Primrose bank on which he lay twined reluctantly in her arms, how he tried to conceal his face, this way, and that way, amongst the flowers, whenever she attempted to press his lips,—

"While on each cheek appeared a pretty dimple:
Love made those hollows, if himself were slain,
He might be buried in a tomb so simple."

She recalled his attitude as he untwined himself from her embrace, and hurried off in pursuit of his steed, which had snapped the rein, that secured it to the branch of a neighbouring oak, and started at full speed down one of the wild avenues of the forest. In fancy she again saw him, as he sat panting upon the ground, wearied with the fruitless pursuit; and how, kneeling down, she then

> "Took him gently by the hand,
> A lily prison'd in a gaol of snow:
> Or ivory in an alabaster band:
> So white a friend engirt so white a foe;
> A beauteous combat, wilful and unwilling.
> Showed like two silver doves that sat a-billing."

And as she looked upon him, she imagined that his lips moved again, as when they said, "Give me my hand, why dost thou feel it?" she fancied she again felt his face upon her cheek—his kisses upon her lips, as when she fell down and feigned herself dead; the while he bent her fingers and felt her pulse, and endeavoured, by a hundred endearments and tender expressions, to restore her. And how, when she pretended to recover, she paid him back again with unnumbered kisses, whilst he, wearied with opposing her, no longer offered any resistance; and how, at last, he broke from her fair arms, and, darting down "the dark lawn," left her seated alone upon the ground.

As picture after picture rose before her of what had been, and every close pressure of the cold, inanimate, but still dearly-loved form, told her what death was, and that those very "hopes and fears which are akin to love," were now for ever darkened and extinguished, she burst forth into such a loud, wailing lamentation, that the sound found its way unto Olympus, and fell upon the ever-open ear of Jove, who, in a moment, dashed the golden nectar-cup upon the ground, which he was in the act of uplifting to his lips, and sprang upon his feet. There was a sound of hurrying to and fro over the mountain-summits, which sloped down to the edge of the forest—of gods and goddesses passing through the air—of golden chariots, that went whistling along like the wind, as they cleft their rapid way—and the flapping of dark, immortal wings, between which many a beautiful divinity was seated. The golden clouds of sunset gathered red and ominously about the rounded summit of Olympus, and a blood-red light glared upon such parts of the forest as were not darkened by the deepening shadows of the approaching twilight,—for the Thunderer had stamped his immortal foot, and jarred the mighty mountain to its very base. And now, in that forest glade, which but a few moments before was so wild and desolate,—where only the forms of the grisly boar, the dead Adonis, and the weeping Goddess of Beauty, broke the level lines of the angry sunset, were assembled the stern Gods, and the weeping Graces, and the fluttering Loves that ever hover around the chariot of Venus. With bleeding feet and drooping head,—wan, and cold, and speechless,—was the Goddess of Beauty borne into her golden chariot, and with the dead body of Adonis, wafted by her silver and silent-winged doves to Mount Olympus. And then a deep darkness settled down upon the forest. Death was to her a new grief; she had seen the sun set from the steep of Olympus, but only to arise again on the morrow; the roses of Paphos withered, but there were ever other buds hanging beside them ready to open; and although she knew that all things change, yet Death had never before seized upon one whom she loved. In vain did Jove attempt to comfort her,—throughout the long hours which wrap earth in night, she wept without ceasing. The stars of heaven burnt brightly around her, but she regarded them not, for those which she loved to look into were dim and quenched for ever. In low tones the mighty Thunderer told her, that all who were mortal must perish, that they must again mingle with the earth from which they first sprang, before they could share the immortality of the Gods; but that when so many moons had waxed and waned, he would, in pity for her sorrow, and for the sake of Love, which never dies, restore her mourned Adonis, but not until the roses bloomed again, which the autumn winds were then withering upon earth. He remembered not, at the moment, that she whom he sought to console had the sole dominion over these regal flowers, that they were dedicated to her and to Love. She had but to wish it and they began to bloom again,—and as she sat in silence, she felt the warm blood flowing slowly through the veins of Adonis,—as the day dawned, his hand returned her own eager pressure, and when his lips moved they gave back murmur for murmur, and kiss for kiss.

When the next morning's sun arose and gilded these silent glades, the Roses, on which the blood of the Goddess of Beauty had fallen, and which were ever before white, were changed into a delicate crimson; and wherever a tear had dropped, there had sprung up a flower which the earth had never before born, and that was the Lily of the Valley; and wherever a ruddy drop had fallen from the death-wound of Adonis, there rose up the red flower which still beareth his name. Even the white apple-blossoms, which he clutched in his agony, ever after wore the ruddy stain which they caught from his folded fingers; and the drowsy Poppy grew up everywhere around the spot, as if to denote that the only consolation which can be found for sorrow is the long, unbroken sleep of death. Thus the Rose, which was before white, became red, and was ever afterwards dedicated to Beauty and Love. And the Lily of the Valley ever afterwards came up with the earliest flowers of spring, proclaiming that Happiness may again return even after the long silence of Death's unbroken, wintry sleep.

The Rose is the queen of flowers, and neither in beauty nor fragrance has she an equal throughout the wide range of the whole floral world. There are now above a hundred varieties of the common or Provence Rose, which were first brought from the East many centuries ago, and from these every species of the Moss-rose first sprung. Even its very foliage is graceful: and the comparison between an opening rosebud and beauty dawning into womanhood, has become a standard and favourite flower in the choice garden of English poetry. In ancient days the bride was crowned with roses; they were suspended over the heads of the guests while they sat at their banquets, and solemnly carried by white-robed virgins in their religious processions. Some of the most admirable passages which are to be found in Oriental poetry, are descriptive of the love of the nightingale for the rose.

Anacreon, in his beautiful ode, tells us that the breath of the Rose perfumes the bower of Olympus, and that the Graces love to twine themselves together by a band of these queenly flowers, and that it was planted, and reared, and twined above the abodes of the Muses; that he himself loved to view it, sleeping upon its glittering stem, in the early glance of morning, to wipe away with tender hand the dew, which lay like tears upon its blushes, and to hold the young buds, while they dropped heavy with the rounded pearls which adorned them. That there is nothing beautiful in nature unless it wears the tinge of the Rose; that Aurora paints the morning sky with its colours, and the velvet cheeks of the nymphs are dyed with the reflection of its blushes. It gives us pleasure to enrich our pages with the following beautiful gem, transplanted from the Land of Roses into our native soil by Miss Costello, and entitled

THE FAIREST LAND.

"'Tell me, gentle traveller, thou
Who hast wandered far and wide,
Seen the sweetest roses blow,
And the brightest rivers glide:
Say, of all thy eyes have seen,
Which the fairest land has been

'Lady, shall I tell thee where
Nature seems most blest and fair,
Far above all climes beside?—
'T is where those we love abide,
And that little spot is best
Which the loved one's foot hath pressed.

'Though it be a fairy space,
Wide and spreading is the place;
Though 't were but a barren mound,
'T would become enchanted ground.

'With thee yon sandy waste would seem
The margin of Al-Cawthar's stream;
And thou canst make a dungeon's gloom,
A bower, where new-born roses bloom.'"

Lily of the Valley! what a spring sound there is in its very name! How delicate it is, both in form and fragrance; resting its white, fairy-like bells upon a deep background of green, like a little child which has fallen asleep with its careless arms extended upon the emerald April grass. Pleasant visions does it recall before mine eyes of other days—of springs which have long since passed away: of old woods just putting forth their summer leaves,—dingle, and dell, and glen, and copse, and many other sweet woodland spots, amid which we rambled for hours together, that were strewn everywhere full "ankle-deep with Lilies of the Valley." Places where the callow throstles first lisped, and the golden-beaked blackbird sang,—where the little wren went hopping from spray to spray, and the yellow linnet warbled forth her song, concealed by the white blossoms of the black-thorn,—they have ever seemed to us as the sweetest and fairest daughters of Spring—the little fairies of the wood, just wakening from their winter sleep,—

"Shading, like detected light,
Their little green-tipt lamps of white."

The drowsy Poppy has been selected, in floral language, as the emblem of Consolation: and, from its dreamy, narcotic qualities, is well chosen. Many of the double Poppies which are cultivated in gardens have a very elegant appearance. It also forms a very beautiful ornament about the borders of our corn-fields, being pleasanter to the sight than to the smell; for the fragrance is very unwholesome, and on this account it is called by the country people the Headache. It is also named the Red-cap, and Corn-rose, in different parts of England. In the heathen fables the Poppy is first said to have been raised by the goddess Ceres, to console her for the loss of her daughter Proserpine, who, while gathering flowers in the fields of Enna, was carried off by Pluto; and ever since then the Goddess of the Harvest has cultivated it amidst the golden wheat. In some parts the country maidens have still a belief that they can test the affections of their lovers by the secret power which the Poppy possesses; that if one of the petals is placed upon the palm of the hand, and when struck smartly makes a loud report, their swains are true, while if it bursts in silence, it foretells that their lovers are false. In allusion to this, there is an old stanza, written, if I err not, by the poet Gray, which says,

> "By a prophetic poppy-leaf I found
> Your changed affection, for it gave no sound,
> Though in my hand struck hollow, as it lay,
> But quickly withered, like your love, away."

In the Apple-blossom we see the Lily and the Rose blended together, like a blush softening into the snowy whiteness of a sweet face ; it may be the countenance of some one that we secretly love — yet dare not, for very fear, give utterance to our affection lest some rival should already be preferred. It may be, at the same time, that we already stand high in her estimation, and yet her innate modesty causes her to shrink back from revealing it ; and so we go on dallying and sighing together, like the spring breeze playing in and out between a bunch of Apple-blossoms, then quitting them until the warmer air of the bolder summer comes forth, and ripens the blushing blossoms into the full fruit of mellowed love. Of all the beauties which Spring hangs upon the trees, as she leaves a wreath here and a garland there, the loveliest of all her rich decorations is still the opening Apple-blossoms — the emblem of Preference in Love.

THE QUEEN OF BEAUTY AND OF LOVE.

Fair Goddess, with heart-searching eyes,
   In thy gold, dove-drawn car descend;
Lovely as when Olympian skies
   Above thy braided brow did bend;
   When Love upon thee used to tend,
And round thy sweet and matchless head
   Did wreaths of richest Roses blend,
Blending the pale hue with the red,
Like cheeks o'er which young blushes spread.

Oh, visit us, fair as when thou
   Sank on thy loved Adonis' breast,
With all the flush which on thy brow
   Did at that very moment rest,
   When feigning death, thou feltest blest;
The while thy rounded bosom rose,
   As does a bird's within its nest,
Hemmed in with buds of snow-white sloes;
When kisses timed thy sweet repose.

Come to us in a cloud of flowers,—
  Around our hearts their sweets diffuse;
Making them like Olympian bowers,
  Where pearly blend with rosy hues.
  Appear as when, through morning dews,
Thou didst thy mourned Adonis chase,
  And he (poor hunter) did refuse
To kiss thy never-equalled face,—
But struggled in thy warm embrace.

Appear as on Olympus' brow,
  When all the gods in love were driven,
And swore, by thy cheeks' rosy glow,
  That every heart was rent and riven—
  That thou wert Love, and Love was heaven.
And that the regions of the blest
  Were unto thee for ever given—
That he who sunk upon thy breast
Would never seek another rest.

Descend as when on Ida's hill
  Thou there didst win the golden prize,
When beardless Paris felt a thrill
  Go through him from thy azure eyes,
  Down-glancing like the morning skies,
When all the world in sleep reposes,
  Saving Aurora, who doth rise,
And to the wondering stars discloses
The couch that's curtained round with roses.

Goddess of Love! it is to thee
All earthly happiness we owe,
All bliss that mortals here can see,
Who at the shrine of beauty bow.
Thou askest but a woman's vow,—
That we shall love until life ends:
Upon our lips we swear it now—
And by each kiss that here descends,
May Hate seize him who but pretends.

FLOWERS OF THOUGHT.

IN SOLITUDE AND SILENCE YOU OCCUPY MY THOUGHTS, SUCH IS MY DEVOTED ATTACHMENT.

EMBLEMS.

SOLITUDE—*HEATH:* SILENCE—*WHITE ROSE:* THOUGHT—*PANSY:* DEVOTED ATTACHMENT—*HELIOTROPE.*

"Juliet leaning
Amid her window-flowers,—sighing—weaning,
Tenderly her fancy, from its maiden snow,
Doth more avail than these: the silver flow
Of Hero's tears, the swoon of Imogen,
Fair Pastorella in the bandit's den,
Are things to brood on."—KEATS' *Endymion.*

"THERE is Pansies," said the sweet Ophelia; "that's for thoughts:" but whether sad or pleasing the immortal poet mentions not. For well did he know that where so many hues were thrown upon the face of one flower, Fancy would, according to the feeling of the moment, trace out her own favourite image. In the dark lines which diverge and widen from the centre, spreading over the subdued silver, branching across the yellow ground of deepest gold, or blended and lost amid the dark hues of the deepest purple. So would the thoughts wander over the one, light and cheerful as the floating silver of a summer cloud, or stumble over the jagged splendour of glittering precipices, like those piled heights which grow golden about the dizzy summits of sunset, when the western slope of heaven glows again with its burning range of up-coned mountains, till over all the dark-blue purple of the evening twilight gathers, and the shadows of night settle thicker upon each other, and all the land is dark. So might the unfettered thoughts, wandering over the face of the Pansy, picture the bright, and the golden, and the dark, which chequer the ever-changing countenance of heaven, as hopes, and joys, and fears, and sorrows, brighten and fade, and blacken over the brief April sunshine of our human existence.

All the old legends which were known about the Pansy in ancient days are lost; excepting the one preserved by Shakspeare, and woven into his inimitable "Midsummer's Night's Dream," wherein he tells us how

> "The juice of it, on sleeping eyelids laid,
> Will make, or man or woman, madly dote
> Upon the next live creature that it sees."

And who that has once read this matchless production can ever forget the pleasing confusion it makes amongst the lovers in the wood!

It was in those days—age of happy dreams!—when armed knights rode forth in quest of adventures, combated with mighty giants, and destroyed enchanted castles by one blast of their loud bugle-horns—battled with dragons, and met with beautiful and disconsolate maidens at the foot of almost every grey and weather-beaten cross, wherever three lonely roads met together,—when the cave of Merlin was visited by all who had courage enough to look into the future, and King Arthur's Round Table was never without a gallant guest,—it was then that they began to seek for signs, and spells, and charms, and tokens, and all the awful mysteries of divination, in the secret virtues of the flowers. But most of all to the petals of tho Pansy did they turn their thoughts, and in its freaked flowers seek to learn their destiny. If the petal they plucked was pencilled with four lines, it signified hope; if from the centre line started a branch, when the streaks numbered five, it was still hope, springing out of fear; and when the lines were thickly branched, and leaned towards the left, they foretold a life of trouble; but if they bent towards the right, they were then supposed to denote prosperity unto the end: seven streaks they interpreted into constancy in love, and if the centre one was longest, they prophesied that Sunday would be their wedding-day; eight denoted fickleness; nine, a changing heart; and eleven—the most ominous number of all—disappointment in love, and an early grave. They called it no end of endearing names; such as Love-in-idleness,—Cuddle-me-to-you,—Kiss-me-at-the-garden-gate,—Hearts'-ease,—Think-of-me,—Three-faces-under-a-hood,—Jump-up-and-kiss-me,—and many others equally expressive, which have yet to be culled out of the pages of our oldest poets; and this flower, eyed like the bird of Juno, has ever been selected as the emblem of the noblest faculty with which mankind is gifted. After all its trivial appellatives are exhausted, it stands up, bold and solemn, the solitary flower of thought: the representative of that silent messenger which in a moment is wafted over wide seas, and to far-off foreign shores; that can recall faces, and forms, and sights, and sounds, at will,—daring even to soar on the wings of a Milton into the presence of the Highest, and to picture the halo of that blinding glory, before which the ranged ranks of Heaven "veil their faces with their wings." Plunging again fearlessly downward in a moment, bidding unfathomable seas open, and fiery volcanoes bare their nethermost depths, while, with fearless eye, it surveys those vast realms where the fallen angels writhe in the sweat of their great agony, amid thunder and darkness, in that fathomless and shoreless ocean of molten flames. Mysterious flower! we know not at what hallowed font thou wert first named,—whether thou wert christened in smiles or tears,—or, amid the maimed rites of some heart-breaking ceremony, wert first named the everlasting flower of undying thought.

The White Rose has long been considered as sacred to Silence: over whatever company it was suspended, no secrets were ever revealed, for it hung only above the festal board of sworn friendship. No matter how deep they might drink, or how long the wine-cup might circulate round the table, so long as the White Rose hung over their heads, every secret was considered inviolable; no matter how trivial, or how important the trust, beneath that flower it was never betrayed, for around it was written the sentence—

"HE WHO DOTH SECRETS REVEAL
BENEATH MY ROOF SHALL NEVER LIVE."*

* Such is the emblem given to the White Rose, in an old work entitled the "Bible Herbal," and published at the close of the sixteenth century—while Shakspeare himself was living.

What faith and what confidence must there have been between man and man in the olden time, when only the presence of a flower was needed to prevent the maligning whisper — to freeze up slander's hateful slime — and destroy that venom which, when once circulated, proves so fatal to human happiness! Beyond the circle to which the expressive text was assigned, that wound about the Rose, not a whisper wandered; the pleasure only was remembered, the painful word forgotten ere it had gathered utterance — or if remembered at all, it was only as having existed for a moment "under the Rose." Truest test of friendship! inviolable bond of brotherhood! Sacred altar, on which heart was sworn to heart, thou didst need no golden chains to bind thee to thy trust,— no solemn vow, sworn but to be broken,—nothing but a simple White Rose to bind these men of true hearts and strong faith together.

The Heath was well chosen as the emblem of Solitude. It could scarcely be otherwise, adorning, as it does, the lonely waste, and waving over weary miles of desolate moorland, where scarcely a tree breaks the long level line of the low hanging sky, and a human habitation but rarely heaves up to cheer the monotony of the scene. It recalls many a wild landscape: the bleak, broad mountain-side, which throughout the long winter and the slow-opening spring looked black and barren, till towards the end of summer, when it was clothed everywhere with the rich carpet of crimson and purple heather, looking from the distance as if a sunshine, not of earth, had come down and bathed the whole mountain steep in subdued and rosy light. The Heath recalls scenes of solitude and of silence — vast plains of immeasurable extent, where only the wild bird flaps its wings—spaces which when the sun has traversed across, the day is ended, and upon the wide outstretched plains you see the night descend; it brings before the eye still out-of-the-way scenes, that go elbowing in where mighty woods meet together, where the bramble trails, and the blackthorn grows, and the red fox sits before the shadow of the steep bank, eyeing her young cubs as they play together amongst the crimson Heath-bells,—spots where lovers might sit and sigh away their souls in each other's arms, without being disturbed by even the foot of the solitary hunter; where the light-footed deer would pace slowly along in his heathery fastness, then bound off in a moment, with all the fleetness of the wind, when he saw the form of man intruding upon his forest habitation,—places where the spotted snake basks securely at the foot of the antique oak, while the long-tailed martin pursues its prey among the gnarled and moss-covered branches overhead,—where the little lizard peeps securely from its hole, and the wild cat glares with fiery eyes from the deepest solitude. Not that Love can ever be solitary or alone, for around it are floating sweet memories, eyes that bend tenderly downwards, that fall sweeter than music upon the ear, and looks that were kindled into sweet affection by the warmth of love.

The Heliotrope, in floral language, is dedicated to Devoted Attachment, a meaning synonymous to that given to our English Woodbine or Honeysuckle, in the language of flowers: it is a native of Peru, and might be well spared from our Alphabet of Love. Its smell is very overpowering in a close room, and as such considered unhealthy. We know no legend connected with it, nor any poem that has been written in its praise; we even doubt whether it possesses the quality from which it was named—that of turning towards the sun, both when it rose and set. It belongs not to the flowers which are twined around our memories—we find it not amongst those that conjure up the days of our youth, when Love but breathed in broken whispers, and the awed tongue could not yet give utterance to the feelings of the heart. Happy days! when even to sigh was a pleasure, and the abashed lips found a rich banquet whilst only feeding upon fancy,—when Love found a May in every month, and the song of the nightingale all the year long in her voice, that never breathed without making the sweetest music,—when, as an old poet, nearly three hundred years ago, in his "Golden Legacy," beautifully said,—

"Love in my bosom, like a bee,
  Doth suck his sweet;
Now with his wings he plays with me,
  Now with his feet;
Within mine eyes he makes his nest,
His bed amid my tender breast,
My kisses are his daily feast,
And yet he robs me of my rest.

"And if I sleep, then pierceth he
  With pretty slight,
And makes his pillow of my knee
  The live-long night;
Strike I my lute, he tunes the string;
He music plays if I but sing;
He lends me every lovely thing,
Yet, cruel he, my heart doth sting."

PANSIES.

"That's for thoughts."

CHILDHOOD.

Sister, arise, the sun shines bright,
  The bee is humming in the air,
The stream is singing in the light,
  The May-buds never looked more fair;
Blue is the sky, no rain to-day:
  Get up, it has been light for hours,
And we have not begun to play,
  Nor have we gather'd any flowers.
Time, who look'd on, each accent caught,
And said, "He is too young for thought."

YOUTH.

To-night beside the garden-gate?
  Oh, what a while the night is coming!
I never saw the sun so late,
  Nor heard the bee at this time humming!
I thought the flowers an hour ago
  Had closed their bells and sunk to rest:
How slowly flies that hooded crow!
  How light it is along the west!
Said Time, "He yet hath to be taught
That I oft move too quick for thought."

MANHOOD.

What thoughts wouldst thou in me awaken!
  Not Love? for that brings only tears—
Nor Friendship? no, I was forsaken!
  Pleasure I have not known for years:
The future I would not foresee,
  I know too much from what is past,
No happiness is there for me,
  And troubles ever come too fast.
Said Time, "No comfort have I brought,
  The past to him 's one painful thought."

OLD AGE.

Somehow the flowers seem different now,
  The Daisies dimmer than of old;
There 're fewer blossoms on the bough,
  The Hawthorn buds look grey and cold;
The Pansies wore another dye
  When I was young—when I was young:
There 's not that blue about the sky
  Which every way in those days hung.
There 's nothing now looks as it "ought."
Said Time, "The change is in thy thought."

THE DAISY OF THE DALE.

YOUR INNOCENCE AND SINCERITY WOULD MAKE RETIREMENT HAPPY.

EMBLEMS.

INNOCENCE—*DAISY:* SINCERITY—*FERN:* HAPPY RETIREMENT—*WILD HAREBELL.*

"When that the month of May
Is coming, and that I do hear the birds sing,
And that the flowers begin to spring,
Farewell my book and my devotion:
Now have I then, too, this condition,
That, of the flowers in the mead,
Then I love most those flowers, white and red,
Such that men call daisies in our town."

Written by CHAUCER *nearly 500 years ago.*

BEAUTIFUL are the fields of England powdered over with Daisies, as Chaucer happily termed it nearly five hundred years ago,—those emblems of innocence — companions of the milk-white lambs —

the first heavings of the awakening bosom of Spring. Majestic are the remains of our old English forests, where around the battered and weather-beaten stems of the primitive oaks, the broad, fan-like leaves of the Fern spread; showing how sincerely they still adhere to the ancient soil which first nourished them, and that, amid the great revolutions of departed ages, they still stand there,—true, but lowly emblems of Sincerity,—marking out the spot where England's mighty forests once spread. There it grew when the maned bison went thundering through the thick underwood, when the wolf made his lair at the foot of the primitive oak, and the tusked boar roamed free from the spear of the hunter. Ages before the son of Acadd came over the misty ocean and called our island the Country of Sea-cliffs, the fern grew broad and green as it does now. And in those solitudes, where human voice was then seldom heard, the tender and trembling Harebell grew, ever waving its delicate cups if the hushed wind but breathed in its sleep Fitly was it named the Happiness of Retirement—the beauty of solitude—the graceful inhabitant of still and lonely places; for when a silence hung over the unexplored depths of our woodland fastnesses, it was still there.

It was one day, after a weary flight from a far-off foreign shore, that Love alighted with a sprig of graceful Fuchsia in his hand, and, sitting down beneath the shadow of a gigantic oak in a lonely forest-glade, he took up the broad-leaved Fern to fan and cool himself, for the air around was hot. Then throwing it down across his bow, he stretched himself upon the greensward, and, playing idly with one of his arrows, he thoughtlessly cut down the blue Harebells and tall white Daisies which grew around him, with the point of his weapon, until startled from his musing and listless mood by the sound of the bugle-horn, and the baying of dogs in the distance, he sprang up hurriedly from his velvet couch, gathered together his bow and arrows, and the handful of flowers at random, and flew off into another solitude far away from the clamorous din of the hunters. It was then that his eye first alighted upon the group of flowers which he had in his hand. On the broad, green background of the Fern rested the sky-dyed Harebells; before these, like a cluster of stars, spread the white Daisies, while over all drooped the scarlet cups of the Fuchsia in elegant festoons; and he smiled as he looked at the graceful finish which the drooping Fuchsia gave to the wild flowers that represented Innocence and Retirement, and the broad Fern that grew up of its own accord, a true image of Old Sincerity.

Through the dew of many a spring morning, ere

the sun had climbed above the summit of the distant hill, while only the skylark beat the blue and vaulted dome of heaven, and with her song wakened the sleeping landscape, had Love wandered forth alone, to watch the Daisies unfold; and so deeply was he enamoured of their innocence, he all day long had often sat upon the sloping hill-side, that he might behold them wave to and fro,—now turning their golden bosses towards the sun, then bending forward and showing the green cup from which sprang each pink and pearly rim, that starred them round like a halo of light. Until the grey twilight would he linger there and watch the buds fold themselves up for the night until they looked like rounded pearls, each placed apart, and when the pale white moon rose up above the dark line of trees that crowned the hill, he would watch the flooded light break over the scene, and breathe a blessing on the lovely flowers while they slept.

Oh, Love! why didst thou not linger behind to see that gay cavalcade pass? for there was a form which thou mightest have mistaken, hadst thou not known her, for Diana the huntress of the woods; for never did the morning, as it looks down upon the thousands of beautiful eyes which open beneath it, light up two such floating orbs of love, as those which glittered beneath that swan-white brow, and swam under the nut-brown ringlets of the Daisy of the Dale. Never did arm more exquisitely moulded or gracefully formed guide the reins of a milk-white palfrey; or forest-nymph more lovely cleave the morning air in her flight, than she who sat, sole queen of the chase, light as a bird upon her rounded saddle. The very hawk which was perched upon her wrist seemed to look into her face with love, and when he hovered high in the air in pursuit of the quarry he needed no other lure than the blue heaven of her eyes to bring him back again to his stand. Even in the banquet-hall of her father's ancient castle, when the stormy and mail-clad sons of war sat around the board, talking of moats they had crossed, and turrets they had scaled, of the lances they had shivered, and the helmets their heavy battle-axes had cloven, if they but once heard her light foot upon the dais, their conversation was changed to that of love, instead of war,—such softness breathed around the presence of the Daisy of the Dale. She seemed like the Spirit of Peace alighting in the midst of those armed warriors upon a mission of Love — as if the white folds of her floating tunic were a more impenetrable armour than the linked mail in which their sinewy limbs were sheathed, and the rim of Daisies which were twined within the silken braid that fettered her floating ringlets, a safer helmet than any that was ever wrought out of steel, three times whitened in the red heat of the blinding furnace: for it was such beauty as she possessed that first softened down the fierce spirit of English chivalry, and tamed the savage grandeur of feudal warfare. Love had before seen her when, sad and pensive, she paced the garden after her mother's death, when the youthful knight she loved was absent, but so wan and woe-begone was she then, that he would scarcely have recognised in the angelic form on the palfrey the

DROOPING DAISY.

Beside a richly sculptured urn,
The Daisy of the Dale was kneeling,
The tears were down her fair cheeks stealing,
And many an outward sign revealing
How deeply her young heart did mourn;
She held a portrait to her breast,
And sighing said, "Oh, be at rest!
Hush, heart! he will again return."

Her glance upon the picture fell,
She kissed the face she loved so well,
Now she turned red, again was pale,
Just like the Daisy of the Dale,

Whose rim is ruffled by the gale,
When red and white in turn are seen,
Coming and going through the green
Of the ever-waving grass.

A silken scarf that lady wore,—
'Twas picked up on a distant moor,
Only a day or so before,
And there the battle had been fought—
A faithful squire the token brought—
The young knight he in vain had sought.
" I wove him this. On this he swore,"
The Daisy said, " I'll think no more!
Dim doubts before my vision pass."

" And yet when I this token see,
And think what nights these wakeful eyes
Bent o'er its dim embroidery,
Painful emotions will arise,
Such as I felt not till we parted,—
Such as but spring from doubts and fears,
And make the bearer broken-hearted,
Through nights of sighs and days of tears.

" Perhaps for me he cares not now,
Nor heeds either my tears or sighing,
Perchance he has forgot my vow!
Forgive me, Heaven! he may be dying,

And no one near! Oh, misery!
Breathing my name with his last breath!
And yet his image smiles on me.
Away!—I will not think of Death.

"No! he will live to wear this token.
Hush, heart! be still, why dost thou sigh?
I will not think his vow is broken,—
I'll not believe it, though I die.
This scarf doth bring back many a scene
Of happiness amid those bowers,
Our walks along these alleys green,
When love was sweeter than the flowers.

"I marked these corners with my hair
I wove his name along with mine,
Letter with letter twined with care,
Hoping that so our hearts would twine;
Oh, Hope! delusive Hope! 'tis Time
Alone that proves thee a deceiver:
Thou bringest buds of promised prime,
But the keen frost attends thee ever.

"Oh! I am sadly altered now,
My summer's changed to winter's gloom,
I've torn the Daisies from my brow,
And hung them on my mother's tomb,

I seem upon a pathless sea.
A lonely ark that still remains,
Doomed to glide on in misery,
And float alone with all its pains.

"Oh! I have loved, and still I love,
And yet my life is like a dream:
I look around — below — above,
And thoughts like hovering shadows seem,
Clouds drifting o'er the face of Heaven,
That float along in loose array,
The dark and bright together driven,
And mingling but to pass away.

"And Love still lives, though Hope is fled,
And Memory that brings no delight.
Telling of Spring, whose flowers are shed,
A weary day long changed to night,
A music all in mournful tone,
Sounding awake, and heard asleep,
A solemn dirge that rings alone,
To tell me I am doomed to weep.

"Though he is false I will not chide,
I feel my heart is all to blame,
And though I may not be his bride,
But see another bear that name,

Yet will I pray that every blessing ;—
Alas! I cannot pray for weeping.
A coldness round my heart is pressing,
A tremor through my veins is creeping.

"Oh! I am weary of my life ;
My eyes with weeping have grown weary,
Nature too long hath been at strife,
My very thoughts to me are dreary.
Oh! I am weary of the day,
And wish again that it were night :
Night comes, I wish it were away—
It goes, I'm weary of the light."

She on that marble urn did rest,
'Twas sacred to her mother's name,
She clasped its coldness to her breast,
She called on death, but no death came ;
The grave is far too cold for Love :
Why should it sleep within a tomb,
When for its mate the wand'ring dove
But coos amid the forest gloom ?

She paused, she heard a distant sound,
Like war-horse tramp it shook the ground ;
The jingling ring of arms drew near,
She drew her breath 'tween hope and fear.

Oh, Mary, thanks! her own true knight
Did from his foam-flecked steed alight.
Though loss of blood had left him pale,
He kissed the Daisy of the Dale.

Her beauty on another occasion saved her father's fortress from the burning brand of the besiegers, when the castle was beleaguered during the wars between the rival houses of York and Lancaster, and when her lover was compelled to mingle amongst the assailants.

On the battlements the cross-bowmen had perished one by one, shot down by the unerring aim of the archers who were assembled without the moat, and whose arrows went whistling through every opening of the embrasures, wherever a defender appeared. The gates of the outer barbican were already carried, the chains by which the drawbridge was uplifted had been severed by the stout blows of a battle-axe, and had fallen down with a thundering and heavy crash across the deep waters of the moat, while throughout the chambers of the inner keep, echoed at intervals the measured sound of the mighty battering-ram, as it threatened at every blow to carry from their hinges the iron-studded doors which swung between the grey old towers; the last defence that stood between the besiegers and the castle. But if every blow which shook that ancient archway went through the heart of the fair inhabitant within, it did not fall less lightly on that of one of the young assailants without, knocking against his armour; while, under the stern eye of his unbending father, he hesitated for a moment to obey his commands, as he stood with his foot upon the scaling-ladder, which was already planted before the tall turret. He felt the wreath of Daisies, that was crushed and concealed beneath the weight of his hauberk, and fastened behind his gorget with a white silken band, biting into his flesh, like so many barbed arrow-heads of pointed steel; and when he had gained the summit, and leaped upon the undefended battlements of the turret, by the strength of his own youthful arm, and the aid of a mighty lever, he hurled back the scaling-ladder with the besiegers upon it, which snapped in two as it fell thundering upon the drawbridge, then lay, broken, and floating, upon the waters of the moat. "Rash boy!" exclaimed his father, as he looked up, the flashing anger of his eye somewhat softened while he stood astonished at so daring and unexpected a deed: "An I once gain possession of the gates, I will put the strongest donjon-keep between thee and that pale-faced maiden for whose sake thou hast done this." But the young lover waited not a moment to listen to what he said, for, flying to the chamber of his mistress he pointed out the way by which she might escape; telling her that his trusty squire and page were awaiting, with swift and surefooted steeds, at the secret postern behind the castle: that it was her alone his father sought to capture, that he might prevent their being united; and so, after a few tears, a few smiles, a few sighs, and unnumbered kisses, he succeeded in carrying off the Daisy of the Dale. The few followers who remained alive sallied with her out of the narrow postern, and went forth without a murmur to share the weal or woe of their beloved mistress; for her father was then afar off, fighting under the banner of his lawful sovereign.

Picture the rage and the astonishment of the old knight, when he had succeeded in beating the battered doors off their hinges, and discovered that the bird he sought to capture had flown, and that his son was nowhere to be found. Thrice did he order the castle to be burnt and razed to the ground; then, before a brand was lighted, countermanded the charge in the same breath: for as he stalked sullenly from chamber to hall, he everywhere met with some object that recalled the remembrance of his youthful days, when, sworn in the solemn bond of friendly brotherhood with her father, they had in their younger years been the first to plunge into the foremost ranks of battle together.

He reached her bower or tiring-room, and saw the velvet cushion, the open missal, and the ivory crucifix,—the coif adorned with Daisies, which, in her haste, she had thrown upon the floor, while over all was suspended the portrait of her mother. And as he sat down in the high-backed and heavy oaken chair, he rested with one hand on the hilt of his ponderous sword, and pressing to his brow the gauntleted palm of the other, exclaimed, "Pretty sweeting! I have done thee grievous wrong thus to drive thee from thy bower, even at the very moment, perchance, when thou wert at thy devotions. Well, well! after all he has but done as I myself would—I have won the empty casket, and he has carried off the prize; and to have won it, the brave young dog would no more have minded cracking my old crown with the scaling-ladder, than a red squirrel minds splitting open a ripe hazel-nut to get at the kernel within. By Saint Swithin! how the mailed rascals tumbled into the moat! I could have laughed if I had not been an angered, to have seen Black Ralph swimming like a duck in his heavy armour; and as for Hubert, my henchman, I scarce could draw the helmet off his ears, so tightly was it fitted on when he pitched with his head upon the drawbridge. By our Lady! he is a bold and a daring knave, and hath as great a love for this Daisy as ever Chaucer had, maugre all the choice rhymes he hath made about it." And the worthy old knight laughed so heartily, as he pictured his followers splashing about in the moat, that his visor slipped down, and he was compelled to call on his esquire to unbuckle the fastenings of his helmet.

Pass we over the long ride of the young lovers, followed by their attendants, through the wild avenues of the forest, the couch which the Knight made among the broad-leaved Fern when the Daisy of the Dale was weary, and the blue Harebells that nodded about her beautiful head while she slept. Love was their guide, and lighted their way through the darksome forest-paths; guiding them over many a wild wold and lonely moor, and beside many a reedy mere, until he brought them beneath the walls of the city where her father was encamped. Wroth was that old knight when he heard that his castle was besieged, and he vowed, by the blood of the blessed Martyr of Canterbury, that from dungeon-floor to turret-steep, he would not leave one stone above the other when he reached the stronghold of his enemy. But when the wars of the Roses were over, the king wrote a "broad letter," with his own hand, to which he affixed his royal seal, and despatched it by a messenger; and instead of foes, the two old knights became friends, even as they were in the days of their youth. And the sounds which startled Love in the forest were the monarch and his retainers, and the two old knights, and their followers, and a great concourse of people, who had sallied out from the castle, and were going to hunt the noblest hart they could find in the thicket, and to honour by their presence the marriage ceremony of "The Daisy of the Dale."

The Daisy was Chaucer's favourite flower; and never since hath bard done it such reverence as the venerable father of English poetry. All worship, saving his own, is that of words only: his is the adoration of a heart which overflowed with love for the Daisy. He tells us how he rose with the sun to watch this beautiful flower first open, and how he knelt beside it again in the evening to watch its starry rim close; that the Daisy alone could allure him from his study and his books, and, when he had exhausted all his stores of beautiful imagery in its praise, his song was ever ready to burst out anew as he exclaimed, "Oh, the daisy, it is sweet!" for his sake it ought to have been selected as the emblem of Poetry, and throughout all time called "Chaucer's flower." For our part we never wander forth into the fields in spring to look for it, without picturing Chaucer, in his old costume, resting on his "elbow and his side," as he many a time had done, paying lowly reverence to this old English flower, which he happily called, "The Eye of Day."

The Harebell we have already alluded to as belonging to the order of Campanula, and it has been well chosen, in floral language, as the emblem of Happy Retirement. It is one of the most beautiful of all our Autumn wildflowers, adorning the sides of woods and shady places with its delicate bells of blue, clear and pure as ever hung upon the azure face of heaven.

It flowers when the dark green leaves that garlanded the rosy summer begin to show upon their edges the waning yellow of Autumn: when on the skirts of the forest, we can trace those pleasing hues which are too delicate to live long, that, like the roses on the flushed cheek of the consumptive maiden, look more beautiful as the hectic tint deepens that announces the approach of Death. The Harebell still blows when on the oak, the elm, the chestnut, and the fir, we see the gloomy green, the burnished bronze, the faded yellow, and the dull red, lighted up between the masses of foliage that glitter like gold, all mingled and blended together so richly and harmoniously, that in the distance we cannot tell where the dusky green of the fir begins, nor the yellow of the chestnut fades away. Then leaves of all hues fall fast, and bury the little flowers which perished amongst the most beautiful that have formed a couch for the declining Summer to lie down and die upon, while other leaves still hang upon the boughs, until they are withered and shrunken by the cold and hollow winds of Autumn, when they fall and bury the Harebell after it is dead.

"While shadows of the silver birch
Sweep the green above its grave."

The Fuchsia we leave to the florist; neither its name, nor the quality it is chosen to represent, have any English sound about them. Taste, saving in allusion to the palate, to us has longed smacked of dilettanteism—it was a good word before so many good-natured twaddlers rendered it common; middle-tint admirers and murderers of Mozart, and pretty verse-makers, have so crowded the temple-gates of Taste, that many, who really possess it, are ashamed of owning to so amiable a weakness, and flatly declare that taste they have none. *Mem.*—Our shaft is only feathered at Pretenders, to which class the fair sex but seldom belong.

The very name of the Fern calls up the forest, where it still lives on, though ages ago the mighty oaks have been felled—there it still spreads, true to its native soil, the hardy image of deep-rooted Sincerity. Even where forests have been uprooted, and the stately deer swept away, still the fan-like

Fern throws its dark-green arms over the spot, unchanged by the changes of long centuries. It is associated with our oldest fairy legends,—creations of some old forgotten poet's fancy, that in

"The middle-summer's spring
Met on hill, in dale, forest, or by mead,
By favoured fountain, or by rushy brook,
Or on the beachèd margin of the sea,
And danced their ringlets to the whistling wind."

And our simple ancestors believed that they had but to find the true "Fern seed," and carry it about with them, to become invisible. What would not a fond lover give for a packet of this fabulous seed, that he might at any hour steal unperceived into the presence of his mistress? But, alas! the secret was carried away with the fairies, when they were driven, with bell, book, and candle, from the green and daisied meadows of merry England.

DAISIES.

"The daisy it is sweet"—CHAUCER.

'T was when the world was in its prime,
When meadows green and woodlands wild
Were strewn with flowers, in sweet spring-time,
And everywhere the Daisies smiled;

When undisturbed the ringdoves cooed,
  While lovers sang each other's praises,
As in embower'd lanes they wooed,
  Or on some bank white o'er with Daisies ;
While Love went by with muffled feet,
  Singing, "The Daisies they are sweet."

Unfettered then he roamed abroad,
  And as he willed it past the hours,—
Now lingering idly by the road,
  Now loitering by the wayside flowers ;
For what cared he about the morrow ?
  Too young to sigh, too old to fear—
No time had he to think of sorrow,
  Who found the Daisies everywhere,
Still sang he, through each green retreat,
"The Daisies they are very sweet."

With many a maiden did he dally,
  Like a glad brook that turns away—
Here in, there out, across the valley,
  With every pebble stops to play ;
Taking no note of space nor time,
  Through flowers, the banks adorning,
Still rolling on, with silver chime,
  In star-clad night and golden morning.
So went Love on, through cold and heat,
Singing, "The Daisy 's ever sweet."

'T was then the flowers were haunted
With fairy forms and lovely things,
Whose beauty elder bards have chaunted,
And how they lived in crystal springs;
And swang upon the honied bells,
In meadows danced round dark green mazes,
Strewed flowers around the holy wells,
But never trampled on the Daisies.
They spared the star that lit their feet,
The Daisy was so very sweet.

LEGEND OF THE FLOWER-SPIRITS.

YOUR FIDELITY AND CANDOUR HAVE WON MY AFFECTION.

EMBLEMS.

FIDELITY—*WALLFLOWER:* CANDOUR—*WHITE VIOLET:* AFFECTION—*WOODBINE.*

Sweet shapes were there—the Spirits of the Flowers;
Sent down to see the summer-beauties dress,
And feed their fragrant mouths with silver showers;
Their eyes peeped out from many a green recess,
And their fair forms made light the thick-set bowers;
The very flowers seemed eager to caress
Such living sisters,—and the boughs, long-leaved,
Clustered to catch the sighs their pearl-flushed bosoms heaved.

BEAUTIFUL Woodbine! thou art the fairest lady of the wildwood—the tall white watcher of the forest! the first to wave thy sun-dyed fingers, and tell to the fragrant flowers which sleep beneath thy feet that the God of Day has once more wheeled up his golden chariot, and unrolled his banner of crimson clouds, above the rim of the distant horizon. Bride of the wood—beloved of the green-waving trees! even the giant oak enfolds thee with a fond embrace, and hugs thee in its iron arms with a gentle pressure. The hooked bramble wooeth thee to twine lovingly between its thorns, and the graceful hazel uplifteth thee on high in its green arms, as if to show thy beautiful tiara of flowers to the surrounding underwood. Around the green elm dost thou ring thy lovely arms, and breathest thy sweet breath in the bosom of the hoary hawthorn, when all its milk-white blossoms have wandered away, or lie withering at the roots of the many-hued flowers of Summer. Over wide solitudes, where the gorse, and the broom, and the fern, stretch far,—where the tangling brier, and the piercing sloe, and the armed holly, bid defiance to the footstep of the wayfarer,—there dost thou sit, with thy fair face looking out from thy turret surrounded with leaves, like a lovely lady imprisoned in some impregnable castle, that stands in the midst of a savage and impenetrable forest.

It was soon after the creation of the world, when the hand of Nature had roughed out its mighty work; had thrown the mountains ruggedly together, and broad-cast the flowers over the hills and valleys, that lesser powers were appointed to arrange them in order and harmony;—when winged attendants were placed over the woods, and fair forms drew out the lines in which the bending watercourses were to run, while the most beautiful spirits, that kept watch and ward over the gardens of heaven, were sent down to superintend, and give the finishing strokes of beauty to the flowers. From many that were gaudy in colour and graceful in form they took away the fragrance, transferring their perfume to lowlier flowers, whose loveliness would have been overlooked, had not sweetness been added to their beauty.

The blossom of the Woodbine was thrown aside pale and neglected, until one fair spirit took it up, and breathed into it an odour which she had brought from the opening blossoms of Eden; another took up her palette, on which was spread out every hue of the rainbow, and gave to the pallid Woodbine a golden and crimson hue; while a third squeezed into its cup a drop of the sweetest honey; and a fourth, around whose slender waist were twined trailing stems of every form, took out the longest and fastened to it the head of the beautiful Woodbine. Tall and graceful did she arise from her seat when she had finished, and twisted it gracefully around her, and as the sun-stained flower rested upon the parted amber of her ringlets she exclaimed, "I will exalt this flower over every blossom of the wild woodland; whatsoever ye plant, it shall still overtop, until its fragrant head is buried and lost amid the green foliage of the trees. All the sweet odours of summer shall float around its feet, and it shall receive homage from every flower of the forest.

"Stop, beautiful sister," said another fair spirit, pointing upward her white finger with an arch look, as she rose from the high pile of flowers by which she was surrounded: "seest thou that old grey naked rock, which stood like a lonely ruin, even amid the silence and darkness of Chaos? for many a day had I looked upon it with an eye of pity as it stood there, grand in its very solitariness, majestic in its own desolation, and looking noble, though bearing the impress of ruin. Hovering around it in the early sunbeams of morning, I thought how its cold aged bosom might be comforted if I threw but a handful of flowers there, and I guessed aright. Sister, look up, and behold how beautifully those wild Wallflowers wave; even the banded bee hath winged his way to that dizzy height, allured by their surpassing sweetness. I will not dispute with thee the tall sovereignty over the flowers of the forest, but wherever a grey ruin rears, though it reaches even to the foot of the low, dark thunder-clouds, there shall the fragrant Wallflower wave,—humble, but high over all,—the everlasting emblem of Fidelity throughout all change."

"Nor shall its influence end there," said the superintending spirit, rising like a tall angel as she spoke, from amid her sister-spirits of the flowers. "I will give it a greater power: it shall stand up like a landmark between the past and the present; it shall recall images of beauty which have faded away, and, throughout unnumbered ages, stand like a sage moralist, proclaiming to the children of men how fleeting is all earthly splendour; it shall lift the mind to the contemplation of an imperishable immortality, and raise the thoughts to another world, where beauty decayeth not, and where the blushing cheek of Happiness is never touched by the pale finger of sorrow. Wherever the Woodbine is seen it shall denote Affection,—the devotedness of a fond heart, that clings unto what it loveth until it dies; but it shall *not* outlive the object to which it is wedded, for, when once untwined from its affectionate embrace, it shall wither and pine, and die away, and be no more. Not so with the Wallflower: when all beside have perished and decayed, when the carved and vaulted roof has mouldered away, when the tall turret has fallen, stone by stone, and crumbled into dust, it shall still wave above the mound of buried ruins, like Beauty bending over, and silently contemplating

Desolation; the emblem of faithfulness in adversity, the garland with which Time shall enwreath the grey piles of silent and untrodden ruins, which in his devastating march he has overturned."

As many of the flowers thus passed through their hands, they gave to them some new charm which they had never before possessed; sometimes varying and mingling their fragrances together, and throwing a warm, pearly flush, over what was before of a pale and deathly hue. They gave a pale blush to the blossoms of the Hawthorn, and pressed the white roses to their cheeks, until they left on them every tinge, from the warm tint of Beauty to the lily-whiteness of their own swan-like necks. Into some of the Violets they looked, until they partook of the hue of their own deep-blue eyes; and others, which were before of a dark purple, they buried in their own snowy bosoms, until they faded into a pearly white, then laughingly planted them again in the ground, causing them for ever to partake of the candour, and sweetness, and innocence of the tender hearts on which they were first nursed, and the gentle spirit by whose purity their colour was changed. Round the Daisy, whose edge before was a white unbroken rim, they clipped the ridge into the star-like silver which it now wears, and called it the Eye of Day. They picked up the smallest Primroses they could find, and, planting them upon one stem, spotted their centres with the deepest crimson, and thus formed the Cowslip. They copied the colours of the golden-banded bees and shaped the flowers of the Orchis after the form of the insect: not a winged butterfly flew past that escaped their eyes:—they transferred to the blossoms the hues of its deep-dyed wings. They swept up all the waste and sweetest blossoms that had blown together, crushing them in the hand until they formed a solid clump of cream-coloured flowers, and so made the Meadow-sweet, that the fields might still be laden with the perfume of May, when the bloom had flown from off the Hawthorn, and resolved itself into one of Summer's unseen perfumes. They made the large Marsh Marigold to plant beside high-banked streams, that in the water the deep gold of the flowers might be reflected, giving them a sun of their own to throw its cheerful and yellow light upon the ripples, in those deep, shadowy, and out-of-the-way places, which the sunshine of heaven but seldom visits. And unto all these they gave presiding powers, emblems, and virtues, and mysterious meanings; many of which Love never recovered again, when he set out on his pilgrimage to visit the Shrines of the Flowers. And ever as they formed the flowers, and strung the beaded buds together upon the stems, and perfumed the petals with odours which they had gathered in the gardens of heaven, their voices blended together as they chanted the lays brought from another world

---

SONG OF THE FLOWER-SPIRITS.

Sister, sister, what dost thou twine?
I am weaving a wreath of the wild woodbine;
I have streak'd it without like the sunset hue,
And silver'd it white with the morning dew:
And there is not a perfume which on the breeze blows
From the lips of the Pink or the mouth of the Rose,
That's sweeter than mine—that's sweeter than mine—
I have mingled them all in my wild Woodbine.

White watcher of blossoms, what weavest thou?
I am stringing the Hawthorn-buds on a green bough;
I have dyed them with pearl, and stolen the flush
Of the dawn from the hills, in the morning's faint blush;
And the odours they breathe of, to me were first given
By an angel I knew in the gardens of heaven:
And Love, should he ever remember the tale,
Shall tell how I perfumed the May of the vale.

Beautiful spirit, why dost thou sigh?
Sad thoughts float about me, like clouds on the sky,
Of the false vows that may on these blossoms be sworn,
Of the Rose that will wither, and leave but the thorn:
Of hopes that may live after Love is long dead,
Like the stem left behind when the flower is shed.
And that is the cause why I sigh — why I sigh —
To think that the heart must be broken, to die.

Sister, sister, what hast thou found
Half hidden amid the green leaves on the ground?
They are the dim Violets, daughters of Spring,
Deeper dyed than the blue of the butterfly's wing;
Yet modest as Love in the bud of the Rose,
When the green can no longer its blushes enclose:
All the perfumes I've tried in the buds that I wreathe,
Yet found none half so sweet as the one that they breathe.

Beautiful spirit, why dost thou weep?
For the death and decay that come swifter than sleep;
For the Rose which my blushes at morn dyed with red,
That by night, in the full bloom of beauty, was dead.

For the beautiful lips they will to it compare,
For the cheeks that will fade be they never so fair:
They are mortal, sweet sister: here Death severs
love,—
Lasting beauty but lives in the gardens above.

The Wallflower is aptly chosen as the emblem of Fidelity, and is commonly found growing amid ancient ruins, when all besides that was beautiful has passed away and perished. For year after year does it fade and blow without the aid of man: we might almost fancy that the spirits of the departed tended them, that over the mouldering battlements, which for ages no human foot hath climbed, the invisible forms of the early daughters of England floated in the still noon of night, and trained these fragrant emblems of Fidelity in Misfortune,—these golden guardians of tower and keep. On many a silent mound, seldom visited by man, have these old English flowers waved throughout long centuries, scattering their perfume over what is now a solitude, but where in former times, hawk, and hound, and pawing palfrey, and lady fair, and youthful knight, and long trains of attendants, gathered with light heart and merry laugh, to start the heron from the reedy mere, or rouse the antlered stag in the forest. To us the Wallflower seems to belong to a bye-gone age.

Nor less beautiful or ancient is the Woodbine or Honeysuckle, with its richly-turned petals, that arch back more gracefully than the broad plumes of the ostrich. It tapers its pale gold and crimson-streaked flowers above the heads of the rugged brambles, ornamenting whatever it clings to, or climbs above, and, like the Violet, sweetens the very air on which it lives. It has become entwined about our rural poetry as a lasting image of Affection and Contentment: is linked with the thatched roof and the rustic porch of the peaceful cottage, over which it keeps silent watch like the sentinel of Love. In one of our old simple ballads the Lover endeavours to entice his fair by telling her that his home is embowered by this lady of the wildwood, and says,—

My cottage with woodbine 's o'ergrown,
  The sweet turtle-doves coo around:
My flocks and my herds are my own,
  And my pastures with hawthorns are bound.

THE QUEEN OF MAY.

HOPE AND DESIRE BREAK MY REPOSE, AND HAVE CALLED FORTH THIS DECLARATION OF LOVE.

EMBLEMS.

HOPE—*HAWTHORN:* DESIRE—*WHITE JONQUIL:* REPOSE —*CONVOLVULUS:* DECLARATION OF LOVE—*TULIP.*

'T was May-day morn, nor had a lovelier day
  From out the eastern chambers e'er been given,
The lark had left the heath and flown away,
  Singing, into the clear dome of heaven;
The bee went round to tell the flowers 't was May.

THE beautiful Hawthorn has been selected, as well as the Snowdrop, for the emblem of Hope; and there are few but can recall with delight the healthy fragrance which has cheered them, while wandering between the green hedgerows of England. Our old poets, as if despairing to find a fitting name for this fragrant blossom, have called it May, after one of the pleasantest months in the whole year; for to them that word conjured up the season of poetry—the month of flowers, and was fraught with associations of all that is bright and beautiful in the earth: for there are but few objects that strike the eye with greater delight than the rural hedgerows which stretch for miles throughout our country, and are at the close of spring flushed over with the pink-white blossoms of May. In the olden time our ancestors did homage to this season of flowers, and went out with songs and music to "bring home May." They erected arbours of green branches, they selected a beautiful maiden and crowned her Queen of May, they placed her upon a throne of flowers, they wreathed her brow with blossoms, and danced around her, and they hung the tall tapering Maypole with gay garlands of variegated colours. Even kings and queens left their palaces, the proud baron rode out from under the dark-browed archway of his feudal castle, the fair lady deserted her bower, and the brave knight, with his plumes dancing in the wind, mounted on his prancing war-horse, rode beside the white palfrey of his lady-love, and so they went forth, throwing their titles and dignities for once aside, to "do observance to the May." Through green winding lanes, and the bridle-paths of old hoary forests, the merry cavalcade went on, singing "How sweet is flowery May!"

Surely we err in calling these the dark and barbaric ages, while they paid such worship to the flowers. Although they might lack the light of that knowledge which has since broken out and illuminated the earth, still they had a fine taste for the beautiful—a simple and earnest adoration for the lovely flowers of the field: and wherever such a feeling exists, whether in the palace or in the cottage, it points out a refined mind, an elegant perception, and a heart alive to all that is pure and beautiful. How natural that so sweet-scented and common a blossom should be selected as the image of Hope! for who could behold it without trusting that there were still better days in store? The disappointed or separated lover, while wandering in the cool shadows of green lanes, would, as he inhaled its fragrance, feel a new kind of joy breaking through the dark despondency of the heart, and hear hope again whisper that the time might come when she, whose presence had hallowed with love every pathway he traversed, should again be his companion, and make those rural rambles the happiest hours of his existence. The fair maiden, pale with love,—the citadel of whose heart had been stormed and won, only to be deserted and left desolate,—might find some comfort while wandering forth among the hedges crowned with May—some momentary pleasure in the remembrance of what had been; and fondly hope that he who had crushed her heart, would return again, sorrowful and contrite, and heal the aching wound which he had made. Amid this sad hope she would send forth a sigh over the landscape, as she gazed upon some thatched and tranquil cottage, which stood half buried amid the dreamy rustling of the trees, coveting so calm a retreat, centered amid the beauties of nature, and surrounded by sequestered paths which led to the homes of hundreds of flowers: for such sweet solitudes does Grief pine for. Such retiring places are sought after by wounded love, who looks for companionship amongst the mute flowers, and breathes her sorrows and her hopes into the listening blossoms, as if believing that the ministering spirits which are sent down to comfort and cheer the broken-hearted, have taken up their abode amidst these green and silent retreats; as if she there hoped to find that repose which has so long been broken, and to rest after her love had been wrecked, on the very shore where she trusted to find such secure anchorage. Nor is the sweetness of Love found alone in the possession, no more than pleasure can for ever exist without the alloy of pain; for as a brief separation enhances the happiness and anticipation of the meeting—as a gentle shower throws a richer odour over the summer landscape, so do the many fears which ever hang like blossoms upon the tender spray of Love tremble before every breath that blows, lest it should sweep off some cherished bloom. And ever upon the ear falls the melancholy truth of "all that's fair must fade;" that Love is ever driven back to its infancy, for, long ere it is permitted to attain perfection, it droops and dies; like roses, which no sooner burst out into full bloom, than they wither; that there is no beyond, no choice but to die, or look back and sigh to "become a bird again," and live over the same brief life: and such is the doom of all earthly love.

It was a clear, bright morning in spring, one of those mornings in which Summer seems to have stepped forth from her golden chamber before her time, as if to look upon her great garden the earth, to see how her buds and blossoms are progressing; when high in the centre of the open village-green, towering above the aged elm, whose weather-beaten stem was surrounded by rustic seats, rose the tall Maypole, hung with gaudy garlands, in which fluttered ribands of as many dyes as there were varied hues in the flowers, amid which they were twined. At the foot of the Maypole stood a rustic throne of trellis-work, covered with flowers and branches of Hawthorn blossoms, drooping in many a graceful form, and on it was seated the Queen of May, her beautiful brow crowned with a simple wreath of wild roses; while, hand in hand, young men and village maidens formed a circle around her, and, with smiling faces, timed their feet to the music of an old-fashioned country dance. At a distance stood the wealthy squire, surrounded by his family, his face beaming with smiles, as he gazed upon the merry group before him, and pointed proudly to his youngest daughter, who sat crowned the Queen of May. For ages past had some high-born daughter of the hall laid aside her dignity for the day, and condescended to preside over their May games. Many a proud beauty who now slept in the dark vault beneath the chancel pavement, on which shone the morning sun, had, in the rose-bloom of youth and loveliness, left her old ancestral hearth and mounted the flowery throne on the village green, to do reverence to May; but never before had there stepped out, from that long gallery of departed beauties, one lovelier than she who now sat the crowned queen of the month of flowers. Her face recalled the immortal sculpture of ancient Greece; and you might have fancied, but for the pearly flush which softened into the peach-like velvetness of her cheeks, and the smile which ever played about the parted rosebuds of her lips, that her head and neck had been chiselled from the whitest marble, with just such a warmth thrown over it, as sometimes flushes the pearl-white blossoms of the Hawthorn. The silken flow of her nut-brown hair was parted Madonna-wise in front, and beautifully broken by the damask coronet of wild roses, which here and there went rounding off, or was half buried in the dark back-ground of her tresses, like a bird partly hidden among the blossoms amid which it sings; a mild, tender light played about the softened sunshine of her hazel eyes, throwing a brightness over the heaven from which they beamed, and a happiness over every countenance, which reflected back the smiling sweetness of their cheering lustre, like the sunshine streaming upon a bed of open primroses, and causing the pale yellow of the modest flowers to "give back gold for gold." Around the ivory pillar of her neck hung a band of rosebuds, beautifully twisted into a silken riband; the warm marble of her arms was ornamented with bracelets of flowers, and the belt which encircled her slender waist was covered with bunches of Hawthorn-blossoms. She looked as if the Goddess of Flowers had newly alighted upon the earth, and ascended that throne to preside over her worshippers. In her hand she held a sceptre, covered with the choicest flowers of spring, and as she raised or lowered it, so the dancers proceeded, or halted in a moment, in the midst of their merry measure.

They also were ornamented with flowers, and had a stranger suddenly come up, who had never before witnessed these floral amusements, he would have thought that the nymphs of Arcady had wandered from their ancient and poetical vales, and come to pay homage to the flowery pastures of England. A handsome-looking young gentleman stood gazing upon the scene, with his horse's bridle thrown negligently over his arm, while he timed the measure of the dance with the butt-end of his riding-whip, upon the ground. The Queen of May lowered her flowery sceptre, and, stopping the dance, beckoned one of the village maidens to approach, when, whispering something in her ear, she took the band of rosebuds from her neck and placed it in the hands of the dancer, who exchanged a few words with five of her fair companions, and they went trippingly up to the young gentleman, and, throwing the wreath of roses around him, brought him prisoner before the Queen of May. Laughing, he knelt down and kissed the white hand which was extended towards him, then took his seat beside her on the throne of flowers. Then again the music sounded, and the light-footed dancers whirled round the dizzy maze, now joined by the jolly old English squire, who made the earth shake again beneath the tread of his heavy top-boots. A few bottles of the choicest wine had been brought from the cellars of the hall, and the corks were drawn by a servant in old-fashioned livery, and, amid loud huzzas, the healths of the King and Queen of May were drunk by the happy villagers. Another dance, in which the queen and her lover joined, being over, the squire and his family retired through the ancient iron gates of the lodge, and were soon lost in the long avenue which led to the hall, leaving the merry villagers to end their May-day game amongst themselves. They elected a new May queen, by cutting a quantity of sprigs from a rose-bush, amid which only one bud was placed ; this, together with the sprays which contained only leaves, was concealed in the palm of the hand, while the stalks or stems only were left visible, and she who was fortunate enough to draw out the rose-bud, was proclaimed Queen of the May, and placed upon the flowery throne, which her sovereign sister had just abdicated.

Alas ! this innocent old English holiday has now all but passed away ; no one now serenades the "sweet slug-a-beds" in the early morning, as they did in the days of Herrick, bidding them rise up and put "on their foliage, and come forth like the spring time, fresh, and green, and sweet as Flora," and not stop to adorn themselves with jewels, for the dews of morning were waiting to cover them all over with pearls. There is no longer that devotion which gave to each house a bough; May-day and May-games are but like flowers thrown into the sea of Time, and cast by the waves upon the long straggling shores, below the dim cliffs, whose heights are only overlooked by Memory. The "Contented Shepherd" lives but in such beautiful lines as we here quote, and which were written by a lady named Mary Robertson, of whom we know nothing, about half a century ago. We place the verses amongst our flowers, that they may not be forgotten:—

"By the side of a mountain o'ershadowed with trees,
With thick clusters of vine intermingled and wove,
I behold my thatched cottage, dear mansion of ease,
The seat of Contentment, of Friendship, and Love.

Each morn when I open the latch of my door,
My heart throbs with rapture to hear the birds sing;
And at night, when the dance in the village is o'er,
On my pillow I strew the sweet roses of Spring.

When I hide in the forest from noon's scorching beam,
While tho torrents' deep murmurs re-echoing found,
When the herds quit their pasture to quaff the clear stream,
And the flocks in the vale lie extended around,

I muse—but my thoughts are contented and free,
I regret not the splendour of riches and pride;
The delights of retirement are dearer to me
Than the proudest appendage to greatness allied.

I sing, and my song is the carol of day,
My cheek glows with health like the wild rose in bloom:
I dance, yet forget not, though blithesome and gay,
That I measure the footsteps that lead to the tomb.

Contented to live, yet not fearful to die,
With a conscience unspotted, I pass through life's scene;
On the wings of delight every moment shall fly,
And the end of my days be resigned and serene."

The White Jonquil, or Poet's Narcissus, is found in most gardens, and is well known by the rich crimson rim which marks the golden cup in its centre. Although linked with the old heathen mythology, and the name of the foolish youth who became enamoured of his own shadow, as he saw it reflected in the waters, still this poetical flower is allied to our true English family of Daffodils, and is often mentioned by our early dramatists. It might have been turned to better use, in floral language, than it is; but being just admissible, and not requiring any over-exertion of fancy to see that Narcissus had a Desire to love some one who resembled himself, we must allow it to pass. The White Jonquil possesses the sweetest fragrance of all this class of flowers, and one which ought to be numbered amongst the sweetest perfumes which breathe from the sweet and parted lips of May.

The Convolvulus, or Bindweed, is known to every one; from the pale pink flower that clings to the reeds of corn, to the long festoons which throw their large, white, hollow cups ever every hedgerow. The Blue Convolvulus, which we see so commonly twined around door-porches, and beneath windowsills, constantly closes its flowers about four o'clock, and such a regular "go-to-bed," as it is called in the country, is no bad emblem of Repose. The Convolvulus and the Briony both twine contrary ways, one to the sun and the other from it; nor can these positions be changed; attempt to alter them, and in a few hours they will either resume their former spiral course, or begin to wither, and soon die. Something very beautiful might be woven out of this fact, and a new legend added to our wildflowers; and had I not given the preference in this group to the May, and occupied my space with a description of its sweetness and beauty, I should have wandered wherever fancy had led me, in pursuit of some old-world love-story connected with the Convolvulus.

Few know that there is a beautiful fragrant Yellow Tulip, which grows wild in our own pastoral England, and which may often be found in full flower, in the warm beds of chalk-pits, about the end of April, or early in May. It gives pleasure to me, a true lover as I am of my own country, to know, that we are neither indebted to Turks nor turbans for the origin of this splendid wildflower, which was, no doubt, more plentiful in the days of our old Elizabethan poets, and which is mentioned in Ben Jonson's "Pan's Anniversary" by the very name it still bears. The gaudy Tulip of our gardens is ill chosen as the emblem of a Declaration of Love; nor is it at all necessary in the floral alphabet, when the Rosebud (a thousand times a more fitting representative) denotes a Confession of Love, and in both cases the sense and meaning are the same. Some have selected the Rosebud as the emblem of a girl,—the language of flowers needs neither girl, boy, nor infant; Love is ever young, and the flowers that denote age grow not in his garden. In our catalogue of the flowers of affection at the end of this volume, we have thrown out numberless weeds which have too long encumbered the flowers in the garden of Love. The Tulip, however, is just admissible, and, like many an indifferent word which has crept into our English dictionaries, must, like the fly in amber, retain its place, because we find it there. Scores of others, which have really no meaning in them, nor bear any resemblance to the qualities they have been chosen to represent, I have rejected with an unmerciful hand, and allowed them no place in my "Poetical Language of Flowers."

HOW MAY WAS FIRST MADE.

As Spring upon a silver cloud
  Lay looking on the world below,
Watching the breezes as they bowed
  The buds and blossoms to and fro,
She saw the fields with Hawthorns walled :
  Said Spring, " New buds I will create."
She to a Flower-Spirit called,
  Who on the month of May did wait,
And bade her fetch a Hawthorn-spray,
That she might make the buds of May.

Said Spring, The grass looks green and bright,
  The Hawthorn-hedges too are green,
I'll sprinkle them with flowers of light,
  Such stars as earth hath never seen ;
And all through England's girded vales,
  Her steep hill-sides and haunted streams,
Where woodlands dip into the dales,
  Where'er the Hawthorn stands and dreams,
Where thick-leaved trees make dark the day,
I'll light the land with flowers of May.

K

Like pearly dew-drops, white and round,
The shut-up buds shall first appear,
And in them be such fragrance found,
As breeze before did never bear;
Such as in Eden only dwelt,
When angels hover'd round its bowers,
And long-hair'd Eve at morning knelt
In innocence amid the flowers:
While the whole air was, every way,
Fill'd with a perfume sweet as May.

And oft shall groups of children come,
Threading their way through shady places,
From many a peaceful English home,
The sunshine falling on their faces;
Starting with merry voice the thrush,
As through green lanes they wander singing,
To gather the sweet Hawthorn-bush;
Which homeward in the evening bringing
With smiling faces, they shall say,
"There's nothing half so sweet as May."

And many a poet yet unborn
Shall link its name with some sweet lay,
And lovers oft at early morn
Shall gather blossoms of the May;
With eyes bright as the silver dews
Which on the rounded May-bud sleep,

And lips, whose parted smiles diffuse
  A sunshine o'er the watch they keep,
Shall open all their white array
Of pearls, ranged like the buds of May.

Spring shook the cloud on which she lay,
And silver'd o'er the Hawthorn spray,
Then shower'd down the buds of May.

CUPID AND PSYCHE.

YOUR ANGER CAUSES ME PAIN, YOUR FRIENDSHIP AND LOVE ARE AN EVERLASTING PLEASURE.

EMBLEMS.

ANGER—*GORSE:* PAIN OR GRIEF—*MARIGOLD:* FRIENDSHIP—*ACACIA:* EVERLASTING PLEASURE—*SWEET PEA.*

"Fly, Zephyrus! on top of yonder mount
My fair love sits; on thy soft swelling wings
Let Psyche ride: you, Voices, that attend me,
Dance in the air, like wantons, to entice
My love to dwell in Cupid's paradise;
Music, with ravishing tones enchant her ears:
She that doth Cupid wed, thus shall she live."

The Queen's Mask, 1615.

In that primitive and patriarchal age, when wealth consisted in the possession of flocks and herds, and the early fathers pitched their tents and made their homes wherever the sweetest pasturage could be found for their cattle, or the clearest streams went

murmuring along through the breadth and length of the sweetest pastoral scenery,—it was then that Love, during his pilgrimage to the shrines of the flowers, chanced to alight in one of those green valleys, which opened out every way beyond the long avenues of venerable oaks, that threw their shady arms over the smooth and flowery plains of Arcadia. Below the oaks spread many a long underwood of fragrant Acacias, of every hue which the queenly Rose wears through the endless changes of her diversified attire,—from the deep crimson to the warm white, as it deepens upward, tint into tint, till you cannot tell where the first faint blush commences, nor trace the almost imperceptible shades it passes through, until it settles down into a deeper crimson than was ever woven into those richly-dyed curtains, which the hand of Evening draws across the sky, when the sun has descended into his golden chamber beneath the ocean. Around the stems of the Acacias gracefully twined every variety of the Sweet, and Everlasting Pea, while their fragrant flowers of white, and red, and purple, showed like thousands of winged butterflies, which had alighted amidst those emerald leaves and curled tendrils, as if to rest awhile, before they sallied forth to visit the green and flowery valleys, which slept in the sunshine on every hand. Whichever way Love turned his eye, to where the greensward spread, or the upland sloped downward to the edge of the stream, he beheld cattle browsing, and saw nymphs and swains attending their flocks, while their low, sweet pipings filled all the valley with music. Here a beautiful bevy of white-footed maidens tripped lightly to the oaten reed of the shepherd, as he sat upon the twisted root of some antique oak, while his flock grazed in the distance, seeming to take no note of the dancers. There, half concealed beneath the embowering Acacias, sat two fond lovers, toying with each other; she timing the distant music with her crook idly upon the ground, whilst he was twisting the Sweet Pea in the clusters of her hair, or hanging its green tendrils here and there amongst the rolling folds of her down-dropping ringlets. Further on a group was gathered around two shepherds, who were contending for a milk-white lamb: the prize stood bleating before them, garlanded with flowers, and they strove, like rival nightingales, each trying to overwhelm the other by the power by its song, as they chanted aloud the happiness which abounds in pastoral life, and sung the praises of the beautiful nymph which each secretly adored. Love stood by unperceived, and listened; and his immortal heart glowed within him while he heard one of them sing the praises of Psyche — the bashful, the beautiful; Psyche, the milk-handed — the star-eyed — the shy fawn; which but the sound of a footstep frightened away. They called her the nymph whose motions were more graceful than the flowers of the Acacia, that drooped and swung in the breeze,—who never spoke but what the very air seemed to hold in its breath, as if to listen to the music of her sweet voice,—who never appeared but the flocks left off grazing to look upon her,—nor ever moved without the flowers bending their heads as if to follow her. Psyche, on whose head the timid butterflies alighted, around whose parted lips the bees flew murmuring, as if they wanted to deposit the honey which they bore to the rich stores that were hidden within them; Psyche, who garlanded the ivory of her neck with the trailing flowers of the Pea-blossom, until the parted buds flew back from her shoulders like wings, as she ran along, followed by the butterflies, when they went out to play together. Love leant upon his bow enraptured, and resolved within himself that he would find out where this beautiful flower of Arcadia concealed herself, for he soon learnt that her abode was unknown to the shepherds, who but occasionally caught a passing glimpse of her beauty.

Over many a pasture and many a plain did Love wander in search of Psyche; through long avenues of mighty oaks, and fragrant arbours of Acacia, parting the trailing tendrils of the vetches with his pointed arrow as he forced his way between them, until at length he came to where a wide field of Marigolds stood, with their heads all turned towards a green bower, formed by the Acacias, and mantled over with the flowers of the Everlasting Pea. Noiseless as a blossom which just moves before the gentle breath of a bird, did Love approach that flowery arbour; and he dropped his bow and arrows in mute amazement, as he gazed breathless upon the vision of beauty which slept in the green shadow of the embowering leaves. Neither the Graces, nor the Hours, who withdraw the golden curtains of the dawn when Aurora rises from her slumber, nor the loveliest forms which hover around the summit of Olympus and wait upon the dreaded divinities,—not Hebe, in whose countenance all the beauty of youth was centered, came near to the indescribable loveliness of that sleeping nymph of Arcadia. And as Love gazed upon her, he knew that he had discovered a form more beautiful than any of the flowers he had hitherto knelt beside.

He listened to the low murmurs which escaped from the opening rosebuds of her lips, and he heard her pray to be wedded to a love that might never perish, to an essence that could never know decay; were it but a moving shadow of immortality she cared not, if even she never beheld the substance of the divinity she loved. "Make me but the remotest point," sighed Psyche, in her sleep, "that forms a portion of the starry circle which the star eternally shines upon, the furthest that is lighted by the radiance on which it waits, feeling itself, nevertheless, as if a portion of that star, although only admitted there like a worshipper on whom the bright effulgence falls. Let me become a part of the lightest down that feathers the edge of an immortal wing, so that I may but feel that I am a part of that immortality; or, if I must perish, give me a brief career of beauty, crowd the space of a year into a single day, and, like the butterfly, send me forth winged,—a divinity floating above the flowers,—that I may before I die taste of the existence of the gods, and catch, like them, the ethereal air, which hath never beaten upon the bosom of the earth."

Love knelt down beside her, and breathing between the parted honey of her lips, in kisses whispered that her prayer was answered; and from that hour she was a partaker of the divinity of Love. "And this power shalt thou possess," continued Love, "so long as thou canst withhold thine eyes from mine; for if once my image is mirrored in the floating orbs of thy beauty, from that moment shalt thou again become mortal, and subject to that death which overtakes the daughters of the earth: for such was the doom uttered by the Thunderer on Olympus, on all who should covet an immortal love.

So fondly do I adore thee," continued Love, "that I will bear thee away to a cave, where Jupiter once sheltered a fair mortal like thyself from the jealous eyes of Juno; where it shall ever be light as noon-day when I am absent, but dark as the hollow of a mountain, into which the air of heaven never breathed, when I visit thee, in all the immortality of my love." Love bore her away to the beautiful cavern which had opened at the bidding of Jupiter, under one of the mountains of Arcadia; and went arching far beneath it: the entrance was concealed under masses of rugged underwood, while all around stretched an impenetrable barrier of gorse bushes, their sharp-pointed spears half hidden by the deep gold of the blossoms with which they were overhung. As a bird bears the feathered seed in its beak, even so lightly did Love fly along, enclosing the beautiful Psyche in his embrace, while her white arm was twined, as if for security, around his neck. A score of times was she about to raise her eyes and look into his face, when she recalled the doom of death which she knew she must endure; and as she remembered the fiat of the Thunderer, she clung more closely to Love, and embraced more firmly the divinity that clasped her in his arms. Once only did she catch a glimpse of his countenance as they passed over a clear stream, and although it was but a momentary glance, she saw in it a beauty which belonged not to earth, and she knew that it was an immortal who loved her.

For many a day did Love and Psyche dwell together in that beautiful cavern, which was roofed with silver spars, and paved with the choicest flowers; while all around were piled twisted and crimson shells, and huge pearls, just as they had grown; and diamonds that, in Love's absence, threw around a light brighter than day. Still Psyche was unhappy, for she had not yet looked into her lover's face. Clear-mirrored, at the end of the grotto stood a fountain, smooth and bright as glass; if she held but one of her silken hairs in her fingers it was reflected back, and in it she could see her own face in the beaded pupils of her matchless eyes. Beside the fountain stretched a bed of golden-coloured moss, and as she had long before persuaded Love not to withdraw the light when he was present, so did she now entice him to repose upon the golden moss, where she could see his image reflected in the basin of the fountain, without drawing upon herself the doom of death. And now she could gaze upon him for hours, with her eyes bent downwards in that clear mirror, while he was so enraptured with her matchless beauty, that his glance but seldom wandered from her sweet countenance; and so imprinted were his features upon her memory, that on every yielding substance she had drawn out the faithful features of Love. He who had eyes for her alone was a long time before he discovered these accurate images of himself, and when he did, his first exclamation was, "What hand hath done this?" Forgetting Love's warning for the moment, she looked up into his face and answered, "Mine, sweet Love! I but copied the image from my heart, where it had been so long engraven, and transferred it there." Love gazed upon her in mute amazement, and whilst he looked, her face beamed with a brightness which belonged to heaven—not a shadow of death passed over it; for she had gazed into a fountain in which the face of Jove had many a time been mirrored, and after the death of Leda, whom he had long secreted in that hidden grotto, he vowed by his divinity, that whatever countenance was next reflected in that fountain should become immortal, nor ever know death. Nor was it until an after-day that Venus discovered this secret, when she found that Psyche overcame every difficulty, and lived on in spite of all she suffered: for never had the Goddess of Beauty dreaded a rival amongst the Immortals until she beheld the lovely countenance of Psyche. Her labours and her sufferings are found in many an old legend; her patience and her tears were known only to Love; and it was during her rambles through the world, while she was driven from the assembly of the gods, that she wandered many a weary mile hand-in-hand with Love, when he set out to learn the long-lost Language of the Flowers.

And ever after, in commemoration of their love, the Acacia was transplanted to the garden of the gods, and the Everlasting Pea trailed about the bowers of Olympus; while the Marigold was changed to a worshipper of the sun, hung with grief, and pain, and sorrow, in his absence, but when present, turning to the God of Day with its golden smile of love. Ages have passed away since the mouth of that cool cavern was closed for ever: for numberless years was it guarded by the angry Gorse, and never durst either nymph or swain venture within sight of those golden-headed spears, after that cavern had been hallowed by the presence of Love. Altars were erected in those valleys, and yeaned lambs offered up to the immortal nymph, whom they believed often came back in the form of a butterfly, to visit the green glades of Arcadia; and many a piece of ancient sculpture, half buried with flowers, has been found in the vale of Arcadia, representing Cupid and Psyche enfolded in each other's arms.

But few of our wild plants are better known than the Gorse, furze or whin: it is a native of almost every common and heath, and there are but few roadside wastes, excepting in low, marshy lands, where it does not grow. We see its bright yellow blossoms blooming amid the dark green of the underwood, and looking in the glare of the sunlight like a bush in flames. Hurdis, in a beautiful poem, entitled "The Village Curate," says:—

> "What's more noble than the vernal Furze,
> With golden baskets hung? Approach it not,
> For every blossom has a troop of swords
> Drawn to defend it."

The Marigold is well known, and there are but few country gardens without it; it is still commonly used as a pot-herb by the village dames. Shakspeare makes it an emblem of grief in the following lines,—

> "The Marigold that goes to bed with the sun,
> And with him rises weeping."

William Browne, in his "Britannia's Pastorals," to which I have dedicated a whole chapter in my work entitled "Rural Sketches," thus marks the close of day:—

> "But, maiden, see the day is waxen old,
> And goes to shut in with the Marygold."

And Chatterton, "the marvellous boy," calls it

> "The Marybudde that shutteth with the light."

There is something very beautiful in the mingled colours of the Sweet-pea, looking as if two or three different flowers shot out of the same calyx. It is like a little ship, with its rounded prow and arching keel, the hull of which is blue, overshadowed with sails of blended crimson and purple dyes. It resembles the nautilus, or looks like a butterfly that has alighted for a moment upon the slender stem, and

"On the flower a folded pea-bloom swings."

THE VALE OF ARCADIA.

It was a pleasant vale in the olden time,
When peaceful shepherds piped along the plains,
And the young world was in its golden prime,
When the green groves rung back their rustic strains,
When the old forest was their only town,
Their streets the flowery glades, their temples mountains brown.

A winding stream flowed through that verdant valley,
And pleasant music its sweet waters made,
As with the drooping flowers it there did dally,
Or, lower down, amid the pebbles played,
Then brawled along through many a mossy maze,
Here lit with struggling beams, there dark with drooping sprays.

And sunny slopes, of green and flowery ground,
Went stretching far along the water's edge,
Seeming to listen to that slumberous sound;
For nought there moved save when the reedy sedge
Bowed to its shadow in the stream beneath,
Or some light ripple stirred the lily's pearly wreath.

A velvet sward, its length deep-rimmed with flowers,
Wound by the stream, and formed a pleasant walk,
Shaded by boughs; sweet summer-woven bowers,
In which the leaves did oft together talk,
Now to themselves, then to the brook below,
Just as the fitful winds in fancy seemed to blow.

Sometimes a cloud, that seemed to have lost its way,
Went sailing o'er the ridge of sable pines,
Steeping their topmost boughs in silvery grey,
Or "glinting" downward on the purple vines,
Till their broad leaves threw back a moon-like gleam,
And then a shadow swept o'er valley, tree, and stream.

Sweet were the sounds that through Arcadia flowed:
The gentle lambs bleated all summer long,
The spotted heifer from the thicket lowed,
The nightingale struck up her starlight song,

A mournful coo the hidden ringdove made,
Now high, now low, now list, just as the branches
swayed.

And Love and Psyche dwelt amid those bowers,
And there he first found how her gentle heart
Drew sweet emotions from the perfumed flowers,
Till of her soul they had become a part;
And how when summer's buds had passed away,
Their fragrance still within her parted lips did lay.

ELLEN NEVILLE.

I AM YOUR CAPTIVE, AND HOPE TO POSSESS SUCH LASTING BEAUTY.

EMBLEMS.

LOVE'S CAPTIVE—*PEACH-BLOSSOM*: HOPE—*SNOWDROP*: LASTING BEAUTY—*STOCK*.

"Why did she love him? she would answer still,
'Is human love the growth of human will?'
To her he might be gentleness; the stern
Have deeper thoughts than your dull eyes discern;
And when they love, your smilers guess not how
Beats the strong heart, though less the lips avow."

BYRON'S *Lara*.

IT was towards the close of the civil wars, when the storm which had long shaken England was somewhat assuaged, and the cavalry of Cromwell had all but trampled under foot the last remains of the royal army,—when wealthy estates were daily confiscated, and the heir of many a noble race slept his long sleep upon the battle-field,—that young Marchmont, who had risen to the rank of general in the army of the Commonwealth, came to take possession of the ancient manor-house of the Nevilles, armed with the broad seal of Cromwell and his Parliament: for the last of the Nevilles had died a warrior's death, and fallen, fighting nobly, at the battle of Marston Moor.

While yet clothed in deep mourning for the death of her brother, Ellen Neville received the commands of the stern Protector to resign for ever the home of her forefathers into the hands of a stranger. A strict inventory had been taken of every article which the house contained, and saving her own wardrobe and a miniature of her mother, she left the hearth of her ancestors a homeless and penniless orphan. The shadows of evening were settling down upon the old park, when, followed by her attendant, Phœbe, she walked with sad heart down the long avenue of ancient elms, in the direction of the lodge. It was still very early in the spring, and, before quitting the park-gates, she stooped down and gathered two or three pale Snowdrops, and then, with a heavy sigh, left the park, while the massy iron gates swung behind her as if with a heavy and complaining sound. She turned round to take a farewell look, just as the sinking sun flashed redly upon the carved escutcheon of her ancestors which surmounted the gates. Phœbe stooped down to pick up one of the Snowdrops which her beautiful mistress had unconsciously dropped, and, presenting her with it, said, "Take heart, my dear lady; this flower is the emblem of Hope, and something tells me that you will yet live to see happier days." The Lady Ellen took the proffered flower, smiling faintly through her tears as she thanked her attendant, then threaded her way in the direction of the thatched grange, in which the honest farmer's wife lived, who had nursed her in her infancy.

Although General Marchmont had risen to such eminence in the Parliamentary army, it was neither by adhering to the strict Puritanic habits of the Roundheads, rendering himself a tool in the hands of Cromwell, nor a time-server to any of his emissaries; for he was one of those who drew the sword through conscientious motives against King Charles, and his own bravery had called forth the thanks of Parliament while his praises had been recorded before the face of the whole army. The mansion which he inherited through a long line of ancestors had, with all it contained, been burnt to the ground by the Royalists, during the commencement of the wars which so long desolated England. Even the very woods which before sheltered it had been cut down for fuel by the Cavaliers when they encamped in the neighbourhood:—all that remained of his ancient estate was the broad lands, blackened over by the traces of the consuming fire. He was one of those who wished to overturn the old monarchy through the purest of motives; who from his soul believed King Charles to be a tyrant, an oppressor, and an enemy of his people; and who, like the noble-hearted patriot Hampden, made up his mind to sacrifice both estate and life, when he rushed into the struggle, to do battle for the good of his fellow-men.

More than one of the confiscated estates which belonged to the Royalists had before been offered to him, as a compensation for the losses he had sustained through the wars, but these he had steadily refused, from honourable motives, when he ascertained that the heirs were still alive, although in exile; nor could he be induced to take possession of the ancient manor-house of the Nevilles, until the most solemn assurance was given him, that not one of the family was then left alive upon the face of the earth; nor did he know that such a person as Ellen Neville ever existed in the world, for she had been educated in a remote part of the country; neither was it long before the eve of her brother's death that she had, since her youthful days, dwelt under the ancient roof of her forefathers. Thus when General Marchmont took possession of the splendid old mansion, as a gift from those who then ruled the nation, and a reward for his unimpeached valour, he was led to believe that he had only accepted what would have fallen to the nation, or, at best, slumbered for long years in the Court of Chancery, until some unknown and undreamed-of claimant had risen up, and groped his way towards it, through the dark and uncertain avenues of the law. So he entered those walls with no other feeling than that of sorrow for the ancient possessors who were dead. Care had been taken to remove all the old domestics, and, with the exception of a parliamentary agent, who had been sent down to take an inventory of the property, no one besides knew that the young lady in deep mourning was the Lady Neville, for she had never accosted one of them before her departure, nor quitted the apartments which had been allotted to her during the confiscation, saving to ramble in the ancient garden.

Ellen Neville was too well versed in the changes which those stormy times produced, to be at all astonished at what had happened, for she knew that she had suffered as others had done who had fallen from their high estate; and although in heart a stanch Royalist, she had heard so much said in praise of the young general,—of his valour, his losses, the sacrifices he had several times made when he thought another would be injured by the offers made to him by Parliament,—that such rumours at last almost seemed to reconcile her to her lot. Two or three ancient footpaths crossed the park, and led to distant villages in various directions; and by the time that another spring had deepened into summer, she had so far overcome her old scruples that, through the entreaties of Phœbe and the persuasions of her old nurse, she now and then ventured out to walk forth into the park; and on one or two occasions had entered the spacious garden, which was endeared to her by a thousand memories, that recalled the happy days of her childhood.

The gardener was a young man, who, during the civil wars, had belonged to the regiment which the General commanded, but had now laid aside his sword and helmet, to tend the flowers, and overlook the spacious gardens. And never would he allow Phœbe to depart, when in attendance on her beautiful young mistress they traversed together the ancient pleasance, without persuading her to accept a splendid bouquet, in the formation of which he displayed considerable taste. Phœbe gladly received the gift, for she soon perceived that the flowers were treasured all the more by the Lady Ellen, through having grown in the garden which from childhood she had ever considered as her own; and thus, while the flowers lasted, they frequently visited the grounds of the old manor-house.

The garden of itself was a picture, too beautiful to be described in plain prose, for near it stood the ruins of an old castle, built by one of the Nevilles who came over with William the Norman. Something like the following, for want of a better, must pass for our description of

THE OLD CASTLE GARDEN.

Hard by the crumbling castle wall,
That old and gloomy garden spread,
With many a quaintly-shapen bed,
And many a mazy path that led
To postern, drawbridge, bower, and hall,
Through gloomy groves of evergreens,
Dark low-browed rocks, and shady scenes,
Hemmed in by fir-trees black and tall.
And all around
That dreary ground
Was heard the sound
Of many a mournful fountain falling,
And many an echo faintly calling
To waving trees and low-voiced streams,
Where Day but rarely spread his beams,—
It seemed a living land of dreams.

There ruined summer-arbours stood,
Mantled with moss and untwined vine,
A wilderness of sweet woodbine,
Ivy and starry jessamine,
And mirrored in a murmuring flood
Were marble forms of many a god,
Some gazing on the daisied sod,
Or half-seen through the underwood;
And Venus fair,
With parted hair,
Was bending there.
She seemed to mock the Sculptor's art,
And listening stood with lips apart.
Others were buried 'mid the flowers,—
Dryads, and Fauns, and Nymphs, and Hours,
Stood peeping through the leafy bowers.

It was one day, while Phœbe was gossiping as usual with the young gardener, that the Lady Ellen had wandered alone down one of the long, pleached avenues, at the end of which stood the old familiar summer-house, where she had passed many a happy hour, when a girl, in the society of her mother: and that, while she sat there musing on old times, and old bygone scenes, all teeming with sweet and sorrowful recollections, she was startled by the appearance of a tall, handsome-looking gen- man, who approached without observing her, so deeply was he absorbed in the contents of the open book, which he held in his hand. Nor was it until the slight rustling made by her heavy silk dress arrested his attention, as she arose from her seat, that he seemed aware of the beautiful vision which thus burst so suddenly upon him. He became mute and motionless in a moment, as the lady in the enchanted chair he was then reading about in the "Mask of Comus," which he had only that very day received, by a special messenger, from the hand of Milton himself; nor was his embarrassment a jot removed when she apologised, in tones sweet as those of an angel, for having thus unconsciously intruded upon his retirement. In the very pains he took to assure her that her presence was a pleasure, and would be so at all times and all seasons, whenever she chose to wander over the ancient plantations, the beauty of which he only regretted were so seldom visited by any saving himself; there was such a tone of sweet persuasion about his voice, such a kindness in the manner in which he invited her to consider the garden as her own, while ever she was in it, and, above all, such an admiration of herself lighted up his looks as he spoke, that no marvel a young lady like herself, who for more than twelve months had scarcely seen any one, saving the rustic inhabitants of the farmhouse, should listen with pleasure to the conversation of one who was every way her equal, and whose name had never been mentioned but with respect, even by the Royalists, against whom he had drawn his sword. With such ease did he glide from one subject to another, that, to the great astonishment of Phœbe when she came up, she found them seated side by side in the old summer-house, he reading, and the Lady Ellen listening with delight to the beautiful passages which he kept quoting from the "Mask of Comus." Many a happy hour did the General and the Lady Ellen afterwards spend together; he remaining in entire ignorance respecting her rank and station, saving that her whole family, with the exception of herself, had perished during the wars; but as any further allusion to the subject seemed to cause the lady pain, the young General kindly forbore to question her.

As the winter approached the affairs of the nation called General Marchmont up to London, to meet the assembled parliament, and during that period he frequently corresponded with the Lady Ellen, for her image was ever uppermost in his thoughts; and no sooner did the early spring come, and he was released from his duties, than he hastened back on the wings of love to the ancient manor-house. The Lady Ellen was walking in the pleached alleys of the garden when he alighted from his steed, and bearing, as he did, about him the marks of haste and travel, he hurried to pay his respects to her before he entered the hall. As he took her hand, he thought that she had never before appeared so beautiful. After a long conversation, during which time flew by unheeded, he looked at the few pale Snowdrops which she held between the whiteness of her fingers, and the small sprig of a hardy biennial Stock, which had flowered before its time, and said, with a smile, while his voice was tremulous with the earnestness of his emotion, "Sweet lady, you now hold the emblems of Hope and Beauty in your hand;" and, gathering a bunch of blossoms from the Peach, which already bloomed upon the old garden-wall, he added, "You are, like myself, well versed in the meanings which the old poets have attributed to the flowers. Sweet lady mine, place this before the Snowdrop, then read me the sentence, that I may know whether or not you have forgotten the Language of Flowers which we studied together last summer." She paused a moment, smiled, looked down, and said, "They mean, I am your Captive, and Hope to possess such——" then she blushed, and remained silent. He confessed his love, and was accepted.

When the General discovered the young lady's rank, he shrank back from his engagement; and dearly as he loved her, from motives of honour refused her proffered hand: nor was it until he clearly saw that their union alone would again establish her securely in her property, and prevent it from falling into the hands of one of Cromwell's favourites, that he could be persuaded to become her husband. "If you love her," said General Ireton, "you will best prove it by making her your wife; for there are already half-a-dozen hungry cormorants ever besieging his highness, and, much as he admires you, if he once perceives your honour leaning too much towards this fair Royalist, he will take up his pen, and at one stroke sweep away the old manor-house, and all its broad lands, from both her and you for ever." Ellen's tears and Ireton's persuasions were too much for even General Marchmont's honest scruples, and the same sun that shone upon the morning of his wedding-day, saw the faithful Phœbe led to the altar by the honest gardener.

THE SNOWDROP.

"Once more I see thee bend
Thy forehead, as if fearful to offend,
Like an unbidden guest."—WORDSWORTH.

As Hope, with bowed head, silent stood,
And on her golden anchor leant,
Watching below the angry flood,
While Winter, 'mid the dreariment
Half-buried in the drifted snow,
Lay sleeping on the frozen ground,
Not heeding how the wind did blow,
Bitter and bleak on all around,
She gazed on Spring, who at her feet
Was looking on the snow and sleet.

Spring sighed, and through the driving gale
Her warm breath caught the falling snow,
And from the flakes a flower as pale
Did into spotless whiteness blow;
Hope smiling saw the blossom fall,
And watched its root strike in the earth,—
" I will that flower the Snowdrop call,"
Said Hope, " in memory of its birth:
And through all ages it shall be
In reverence held, for love of me."

"And ever from my hidden bowers,"
  Said Spring, "it first of all shall go,
And be the herald of the flowers,
  To warn away the sheeted snow:
Its mission done, then by thy side
  All summer long it shall remain.
While other flowers I scatter wide,
  O'er every hill, and wood, and plain,
This shall return, and ever be
A sweet companion, Hope, for thee."

Hope stooped and kissed her sister Spring,
  And said, "For hours, when thou art gone,
I'm left alone without a thing
  That I can fix my heart upon;
'Twill cheer me many a lonely hour,
  And in the future I shall see
Those who would sink raised by that flower,—
  They'll look on it, then think of thee:
And many a sadful heart shall sing,
The Snowdrop bringeth Hope and Spring."

TIME AND THE FLOWERS.

YOUR YOUTHFULNESS CAUSES ME TO FEAR THAT YOU MAY CHANGE: ONCE UNITED I SHALL BE NO LONGER PENSIVE.

EMBLEMS.

YOUTHFULNESS—*CROCUS:* CHANGE—*PIMPERNEL:* UNITED—*LANCASTER ROSE:* PENSIVENESS—*COWSLIP.*

"'Twas a happy thought to mark the hours
By the opening and the folding flowers;
Yet is not life in its real flight
Marked even thus on earth,
By the closing of one Hope's delight,
Ere another Hope hath birth?"

MRS. HEMANS.

HAPPY was that age, when Love and Beauty kept no other record of time than what they found in the opening and closing of the flowers,—when the day was measured by the rising and setting of the sun, and the hours marked in the unfolding

and shutting of the blossoms. Morning and evening the village maiden marked the hour of milking-time, by the waking and sleeping of the Daisy. The mower, as he strode forth, with his scythe over his shoulder, to cut down the summer flowers, hastened his step if he saw that the cup of the Convolvulus had expanded; and when his arm was weary, turned to the hedge, over which it trailed in many a fantastic line, for the close of his day's labour was announced by the shutting of the Bindweed. The rustic beauty, before she went forth to Wake or Feast, or donned her holiday attire, went out and peeped at the scarlet Pimpernel; and if its starry petals were closed, she knew that the showers would soon descend, and, sighing, laid aside her Sunday garments, until she could see the purple spot at the bottom of the scarlet flower.

They knew that Winter was awakening from his long sleep when the Snowdrop and the Crocus appeared; they dated the coming of Spring from the yellow dawning of Primroses upon the banks, and the deep flush of Violets which lay like a purple cloud upon the grass; and when the Roses and Honeysuckles were in full bloom, they knew that Summer had come in the beauty of her broad bloom of flowers; but, when only a blossom was seen here and there upon the Bramble, and the blue of the nodding Harebell looked wan and pale, and the crimson flush of the hardy Heath had faded from its cheek, they whispered that the solemn Autumn was at hand: for a thousand varied hues proclaimed that the funeral pyre of Summer was kindled, and all her flowers faded away to the ashy grey, which only remains behind, when all her beauty is extinguished.

Then Childhood sallied forth, with merry shout and happy heart, and ran, until it was compelled to stop through sheer weariness, to and fro among the unnumbered flowers; shaking off, in its eager flight, the loosened silver from the Daisy, and the dusty gold from the deep yellow of the Buttercup. Young lovers only numbered the many happy meetings they had had together by the days which the milk-white Hawthorn remained in blossom, and the many times they had heard the song of the cuckoo, while seated beneath its fragrant shade. Old Age dated the years it had lived by recalling how many times it had seen the Wild Rose blow, and wandered forth to gather the spotted blossoms of the golden Cowslip. They kept their records of marriages by the flowers which then bloomed, and the solemn memory of the dead by the fragrant blossoms which they showered upon their graves. They recalled their joys and sorrows by the seasons, and dated their success or adversity by the coming in or going out of the flowers. Not that the flapping of Time's grey wings sounded the less solemnly upon their ears, or the waving of his hoary plumes passed the less unnoticed, because they beat only upon a race who recorded his flight by the sleeping and awakening of the buds. No! it prepared them for the great change which they knew would some day take place; and they looked forward to their journey to another world with a saddened pleasure, deepened the more by the remembrance of the beautiful flowers they were compelled to leave behind, and half fearing that they might never love those so well, which would bloom for ever, in that land of eternal light beyond the grave.

They knew not the empty love, in which the heart is no partaker,—the vows which they breathed were intended to reach heaven, and to be registered there amid all other holy things: for to them the Accusing Spirit was not an empty name—they believed that its All-seeing eye kept a severe watch over the plighted troth of Love, and that the Recording Angel never blotted out a single letter which stood beside his name who had broken the heart of a fond and confiding woman. Wealth had not then ploughed down and dug out that deep abyss, every foot of which separates us further from heaven: man wandered not in those days in the dark, amid stumbling-blocks and wedges of unfeeling gold; he moved not in that cold, cheerless atmosphere, where Love would never be able to breathe, and Affection could never open the smallest of its beautiful buds. For in that heart which pines only for riches, Love can, at best, but find only a brief dwelling-place—no blossom can ever come into full bloom amid such darkness! Mammon alone dwells there: he is the sole god of those cheerless dominions, and ever doth he sit alone with his aching head pillowed upon a wedge of gold. The cold, faint light of the unfeeling riches that surround him makes him shiver—he can find no warmth in his bright icy diamonds—he freezes in his mail of silver—and when it is too late, learns that the warm and beating heart of a loving woman is the richest gem that the angels ever dropped into the world; that without her Happiness cannot exist: that there is no true Love where she is not: that real Friendship lives nowhere long, unless nursed within her gentle breast: that when tender Pity returned to heaven, she threw her mantle over the white shoulders of woman, and bade her ever wear it for her sake: that Sorrow and Sincerity pressed her lips ere they soared away together, hand in hand; they left her not hidden by a curtain of gold, but kneeling with her long hair unbound, and her white supplicating hands uplifted, praying for some one to come and comfort her. That after a time an angel, with averted head, led forth man, then turned away weeping and silent : and all night, as he stood alone, sorrowing, beside the battlements of heaven, his immortal heart smote him for what he had done.

It was one day, as Time sat musing in the midst of his ruins, while his scythe lay idly by his side, and he took no notice of the glass, as through it ebbed slowly the ever-moving sand, that his thoughts turned to the cities he had laid low, and the countries over which he had marched, through many a bygone century. Much he marvelled within himself that the scenes which he had ages ago made desolate, should, in spite of his inroads, have again recovered their beauty, and in place of the solitude and dreariment which he had left behind, be fragrant with the breath of thousands of flowers, and alive with the hum and murmuring of bees. "I will destroy the flowers," said Time; "they rob all my ruins of their solemnity, and no one can think of desolation wherever they are seen to wave: before me they spring up, and behind me they arise in the very footsteps where I have left the marks of death, decay, and desolation: they bloom in the silent aisles of the very abbeys which I have unroofed; and where I have swept away every trace of the massy and ornamented roofs of the dead, there they come and wave." And as he sat upon the base of the ruined column, he began to sharpen his scythe; but just as he was about to commence the work of destruction, one of the wandering Spirits of the Flowers rose up before him, and placed her hand upon his arm. "Wilt thou spoil the beauty of thine own workmanship?" said the fair Spirit of the Blossoms: "what greater victory wouldst thou wish to win over the power of man, than that which thou hast already obtained? Thou passest over his mighty works, and they crumble at thy touch into the dust: thou hast but to sit down and look upon the masses of masonry which he has piled together, and, beneath thy silent gaze, they moulder slowly away. It is over thy workmanship that we scatter the flowers, to show that thou hast ended what he but began; we but pile up a monument on those silent shores, where the pride of man is wrecked. Would thy work be less complete if all was blank and desolate? would weary leagues of brown and barren land show the traces of thy power? or would they not look like spots over which thy wings had never waved? It is the peace and beauty which again reign over the places thy hand hath made desolate, that hallow the solitude, and point out that, although Nature cannot restore what thou hast overthrown, she can still beautify what remains behind."

Time mused a moment, then took up his scythe and hurried away, leaving the beautiful Spirit to do as she willed with the flowers.

And ever since that period they have grown about the grey ruins which Time hath left behind, and waved upon the roofless walls which have decayed beneath his mouldering touch, and would, long ago, have crumbled into dust, but for the flowers, which held the weather-beaten battlements together. Over many a mound, beneath which the foundations of forgotten abbeys lie buried, does the crimson-spotted and pensive Cowslip still wave, and the early Crocus unfold its golden sheath to catch the cheering sunshine of Spring. To Time was given power over the works of man, but over those of Nature he holds no sway; from the very flowers that perish others as beautiful spring up, and the oak sheds the acorns from which arise other trees. Temples and palaces he overturns, and they are no more; nor can we ever know the forgotten graves which he has obliterated, and trampled into the dust. In the undated summers of the past, Youth and Beauty wandered over the same flowery meadows which we delight in rambling over now; sunshine and shadow swept above the long grass; and flowers, like those we still look upon, bowed idly in the breeze before their eyes, as they still do before our own. Could they traverse the same spots again in the coming summer, saving the altered hedgerow, and the rustic stile, they would behold no change: the Crocus, and the Cowslip, the Bluebell, Buttercup, and Daisy, would stand dreaming among the green grass, as they did a thousand years ago; the hoary Hawthorn would throw out as sweet a fragrance, and the hidden Violet betray the bed where its blue sisters slept, by the delicacy of its unaltered perfume: for Time has not left a trace of his footmarks upon the flowers. The same sunshine which lighted up the silver of the Daisy, and deepened the pale gold of the Primrose, when Chaucer went forth to do "observance to the May," sleeps upon them in the sweet spring-time of our own days; and although the Poet would find no traces of the castles in which he was ever a welcome guest, his favourite flowers would be there to greet him with a silent welcome, as they did in the days of old when he went forth to listen to the song of the nightingale. And those Roses which, between the wars of the rival houses of York and Lancaster, caused blood enough to be spilt to make the white for ever red, would be found blowing, as peacefully in a few old gardens, as if the blast of war had never been heard in the world; bearing about them no trace of the strife and the struggle, which the grave has for ever hushed, nor a mark of the finger of Time upon the unsullied bloom of their buds. Nor could the eye that then beheld them, tell that a flower had changed : for as they looked on the morning of battle, and on the evening of the same day, when the sun sank over a field crimson with blood, so do they look now ; the keen eye of Time, who discerneth the decay of all things, seeth change in the flowers.

The fond, warm heart of lovely woman ceaseth to beat — the liquid ruby no longer danceth through the streaked violets of her blue veins — the opening roses of her sweet and parted lips are closed for ever — the silver melody of her harp-toned voice is heard no more — the heaven of her eyes, the loveliest mirror in which the face of man was ever imaged, is darkened — and she, the most beautiful flower that was ever formed by the hand of Heaven, sleeps unconsciously below ; while the flowers bloom and fade a thousand times above her grave, yet their beauty cheereth not, neither doth their perfume gladden, the angel of earth that slumbereth beneath. Over the blossoms above Time hath no power : but the sweet bud which lieth buried deep down, belongeth for a season unto him and Death, and to us can never again be restored. And what careth Time for other flowers ? he carrieth away those which are twined around our hearts, — he teareth the bleeding tendrils asunder : the vast cities and huge temples are not his only prey, for from the beginning he became a partner with Death, and they have ever since divided all but the flowers between them.

But let us not mourn: for from that hour when the spirit of Abel went wailing over the bowers of Eden, in the dim twilight of the early world, were the immortal gates of heaven thrown open; and Time and Death looked aghast upon each other, as they heard those golden doors swing wide, and caught a glimpse of the first mortal that passed through the cold gates of Death to that bright abode of eternal sunshine, and those boundless gardens filled with never-dying flowers. From that moment they knew that their power extended not beyond the grave; that but for a brief space the beauty of mortality should close, like a flower that folds itself up and sleeps, while all the land around is dark, then opens again beneath a new morning, which had never before dawned upon the world; whose golden beams would throw around it an immortal halo, and give neither Time nor Death again power over the drooping bud which those sun-rays had touched. It was then that Love alighted upon the earth, and proclaimed to all that the hearts which remained true and faithful to each other should be united again after death; that true love was immortal, and could never perish; that on this cold, changeable earth, Happiness never arrived to its pure perfection; for here Love was ever in its infancy, chilled by the fear of Death, and nipped by the biting winds of sorrow; and that those who treasured a true, unchanged, and devoted heart through all these trials, should hereafter enjoy an unbroken eternity of Love. And Love pointed to the flowers, which the rains of Autumn beat down and the bleak winds of Winter blew upon, showing how, through all these trials, they struggled and sprung up into a new life,—fairer than before they faded, sweeter than when they perished; and that such should be the reward hereafter for those who endured without repining; who waited and served in patience, whom neither prosperity nor adversity could change, but went on for ever loving unto the end, and proving that "love is love for evermore." That for all such were immortal garlands woven in the gardens above,—over which neither Death nor Time had power: for they bore within them a divinity that never could be affected by Time, nor perish, even for a brief space, like the flowers.

THE HAPPY VALLEY.

It was a valley filled with sweetest sounds,
A languid music haunted everywhere,
Like those with which a summer-eve abounds,
From rustling corn and song-birds calling clear.
Down sloping uplands, which some wood surrounds,
With tinkling rills, just heard, but not too near,
And low of cattle on the distant plain,
And peal of far-off bells, now caught, then lost again.

It seemed like Eden's angel-peopled vale,
So bright the sky, so soft the streams did flow;
Such tones came riding on the musk-winged gale,
The very air seemed sleepily to blow;
And choicest flowers enamelled every dale,
Flushed with the richest sunlight's rosy glow:
It was a valley drowsy with delight,
Such fragrance floated round, such beauty dimmed the sight.

The golden-belted bees hummed in the air,
  The tall, silk grasses bent and waved along;
The trees slept in the sleeping sunbeam's glare,
  The dreamy river chimed its undersong,
And took its own free course without a care:
  Amid the boughs did lute-tongued songsters throng,
And the green valley throbbed beneath their lays,
While Echo Echo chased through many a leafy maze.

Sweet shapes were there, the Spirits of the Flowers,
  Sent down to see the Summer-beauties dress,
And feed their fragrant mouths with silver showers;
  Their eyes peeped out from many a green recess,
And their fair forms made light the thick-set bowers;
  The very flowers seemed eager to caress
Such living sisters; and the boughs, long-leafed,
Clustered to catch the sighs their pearl-flushed bosoms heaved.

One through her long loose hair was backward peeping,
  Or throwing, with raised arm, the locks aside;
Another high a pile of flowers was heaping,
  Or looking love askance, and, when descried,
Her coy glance on the bedded-greensward keeping;
  She pulled the flowers to pieces as she sighed,
Then blushed like timid daybreak, when the dawn
Looks crimson on the night, and then again's withdrawn.

One, with her warm and milk-white arms outspread,
On tip-toe tripped along a sunlit glade;
Half turned the matchless sculpture of her head,
And half shook down her silken circling braid:
She seemed to float on air, so light she sped;
Her back-blown scarf an archèd rainbow made.
She skimmed the wavy flowers as she passed by,
With fair and printless feet, like clouds along the sky.

One sat alone within a shady nook,
With wildwood songs the lazy hour beguiling;
Or looking at her shadow in the brook,
Trying to frown, then at the effort smiling—
Her laughing eyes mock'd every serious look;
'Twas as if Love stood at himself reviling:
She threw in flowers, and watched them float away,
Then at her beauty looked, then sang a sweeter lay.

Others on beds of roses lay reclined,
The regal flowers athwart their full lips thrown,
And in one fragrance both their sweets combined,
As if they on the self-same stem had grown:
So close were rose and lip together twined,
A double flower that from one bud had blown,
Till none could tell, so sweetly were they blended,
Where swelled the curving lip, or where the rose-bloom ended.

One, half asleep, crushing the twinèd flowers,
Upon a velvet slope like Dian lay;
When she within the twilight forest cowers;
Her looped-up tunic, tossed in disarray,
Showed rounded limbs too fair for earthly bowers—
They looked like roses on a cloudy day,
The warm white dulled amid the colder green;
The flowers too rough a couch that lovely shape to screen.

Some lay like Thetis' nymphs along the shore,
With ocean-pearl combing their golden locks,
And singing to the waves for evermore;
Sinking like flowers at eve beside the rocks,
If but a sound, above the muffled roar
Of the low waves, was heard. In little flocks
Others went trooping through the wooded alleys,
Their kirtles glancing white, like streams in sunlit valleys.

They were such forms as, imaged in the night,
Sail in our dreams across the heaven's deep blue;
When the closed lid sees visions streaming bright,
Too beautiful to meet the naked view,
Like faces formed in clouds of silver light:
Women they were! such as the angels knew—
Such as the Mammoth looked on, ere he fled,
Scared by the lovers' wings, that streamed in sunset red.

INDEX

OF THE

POETICAL LANGUAGE OF FLOWERS.

ABSENCE—*Wormwood.* Its derivation signifies, without sweetness; and so far may Absence be put down as the bitterness of Love.

ACCOMMODATING DISPOSITION—*Red Valerian.* Will grow on old walls, ruins, or almost anywhere; hence its floral signification.

AFFECTIONATE REMEMBRANCE—*Rosemary.* "That's for Remembrance: I pray you, love, remember;" says the sweet Ophelia. And who would wish to change the emblem of a flower which Shakspeare has made immortal?

AFTER-THOUGHT—*Michaelmas Daisy.* Which blows when the flowers of summer have faded: coming unaware, like a pleasant thought.

AMIABILITY—*White Jasmine.* Its sweetness, and beauty, and star-like flowers, bear about them a resemblance to an amiable lady. Gilbert White saw this in the drooping form of the silver-stemmed Birch, when he called it the "Lady of the Wood." He would have added "Amiable," had it been starred with beautiful flowers like the Jasmine.

ANGER—*Gorse, Furze, or Whin.* A pretty, though formidable plant, armed up to the very gold of the flowers, and piercing those who approach not its beauty carefully.

ARTS—*Acanthus.* Worthily placed in honour of Callimachus, who is said to have formed from its beauty the capital of the Corinthian column, as he saw it growing over the grave of a young maiden.

ASSIGNATION—*Pimpernel.* Its regularity in opening and shutting is well selected as denoting an appointment between lovers, who are supposed to trust more to the bright sunshine and sweet flowers, and the feelings of their own hearts, than the measured minutes of Time. It also denotes change in the weather, as the flowers always close before rain. By country people it is called the Shepherd's Weather-glass.

BASHFULNESS—*The Maiden's Blush Rose.* One of the most beautiful and delicate of all the queenly class of roses.

BEAUTY—*The Rose.* Its very name is beautiful: and more than two thousand years ago it was worshipped by the poets, and called the Queen of Flowers.

BELIEF—*Passion Flower.* Has become strangely woven with our faith, from a fancied resemblance to a cross and a crown, although it requires a great effort of the imagination to call up either the one or the other. Still its very name, in some measure, renders it sacred to Faith and Belief.

CANDOUR—*White Violet.* See "Legend of the Flower-Spirits," page 110.

CHASTITY—*Orange Blossom.* These flowers are commonly worn now by the young bride; though we know not why the Orange-blossom was selected as the emblem of Chastity. The custom of wearing it at weddings, we believe, first originated in France.

CONFESSION—*Moss-rosebud.* A beautiful and poetical representation of the first confession of love, and so alluded to by our old poets; Rosebuds having for ages been emblems of youthful love.

CONSOLATION—*Poppy*. Denotes sleep, rest, repose: all of which are well represented in its drowsy properties and influence.

CONSTANCY—*Canterbury-bell*. Which we have already described. See "Old Saxon Flowers," pages 53–55.

COQUETRY—*Yellow Day Lily*. Called by the French "the Beauty of a Day;" who reigning, as she generally does, over so many admirers, coquettes with all without loving one.

CRUELTY—*Stinging Nettle*. Wounds the hand that presses it ever so gently. However dull the comprehension of a lover might be, he could not well fail to understand the meaning of this plant.

DECEITFUL CHARMS—*Thorn Apple*. A gorgeous shrub, scarcely equalled in beauty, although its perfume is considered unhealthy; hence its meaning in floral language.

DECLARATION OF LOVE—*Tulip*. So received: though far inferior to the Rosebud as an emblem of the tender passion.

DELICACY—*Bluebottle*. A beautiful flower that grows in the corn-fields, and is second to none in the delicacy of its colouring.

DESERTION—*Love-lies-Bleeding*. Like the Forget-me-Not, conveys a meaning in its very name.

DESIRE—*Jonquil*, or *Poet's Narcissus*. See Legend of the "Queen of May," page 126.

DEVOTED AFFECTION—*Honeysuckle* or *Woodbine*. A beautiful adaptation of a sweet wild flower to a poetical sentence, and called by the French the "Links of Love," from its clinging to the object it adorns. See "Legend of the Flower-Spirits," pages 107, 108.

DEVOTED ATTACHMENT—*Heliotrope*. See "Flowers of Thought," page 80.

DIFFICULTY—*Blackthorn.* Which is so armed with sharp and piercing thorns, that it is difficult to gather the blossoms without tearing the hand.

DISAPPOINTED LOVE—*Willow.* Shakspeare made Othello's maid, poor Barbara, go about the house hanging her head aside, and singing, "Oh, willow, willow!" for he she loved proved false.

DISSENSION—*The Stalk from which the Flower is broken off.* This is a better emblem than a broken straw, and more expressive.

DOUBT—*Blossom of the Apricot.* Which requires gentle rains, and warm, bright, sunshiny weather, to bring the fruit to perfection. Any other delicate blossom would have been as applicable an emblem.

ELEGANCE—*Acacia.* There is something about the form of these beautiful flowers, as they droop and wave in the breeze, that conveys an idea of elegance and neatness, without being gaudy. They conjure up the image of a lady chastely and not garishly attired. The Yellow Acacia is also the emblem of Friendship.

ENCHANTMENT—*Vervain.* Supposed to have been used by the wizards of old in their spells, omens, &c.; but that power is now transferred to the bewitching face of woman, for that is the true enchanter of modern times.

ENVY—*Bramble.* Tears and rends everything it clings to, and is the dread of fair ladies who venture to ruralise in old forests, thick with underwood. The Brier and Thorn are old emblems of Pain, Envy, and Suffering, and are frequently alluded to by our poets. Burns, in his "Banks o' Doon," says,—

> "And my false lover stole the rose,
> But ah! he left the thorn with me."

ESTEEM—*Sage.* So called, no doubt, in floral language, because the sages and philosophers of old were held in high esteem for their gravity and wisdom.

EVERLASTING PLEASURE—*Sweet Pea*. See Legend of "Cupid and Psyche," page 133.

FALSEHOOD—*Deadly Nightshade*. The fruit of which produces poison and death, and cannot be pointed out too soon to the innocent and unwary, that they may be prevented from gathering it.

FIDELITY IN MISFORTUNE—*Wallflower*. A beautiful emblem. See "Legend of the Flower-Spirits," pages 108, 109.

FIRST EMOTIONS OF LOVE—*Lilac*. Its fragrance and the fresh and healthy look of its blossoms, which are amongst the first to unfold in the spring, are well chosen as the representatives of early love.

FORESIGHT—*Dandelion*. The schoolboy's clock and oracle in every village: for who, when young, has not blown its tufted down away, and at every breath sent a wish after the feathered seeds of the Dandelion?

FORGET-ME-NOT—*Forget me not*. Nothing can be more expressive than its name. See page 16, and Poem, page 24.

FORSAKEN—*Primrose*. We have selected the Primrose in honour of Milton, who says, "And the rathe Primrose that *forsaken* dies;" and for the sake of the Bard of Paradise such a meaning ought it ever to bear, instead of the Anemone.

FRIENDSHIP—*Ivy*. Denotes something true and lasting, and not to be changed by the beating of the wintry winds. It is a much better emblem of Friendship than the Acacia, which some have chosen, and as such is used by our early poets·

GLORY—*Laurel.* Was used by the ancients to crown those heroes who returned from the wars victorious. Chaucer, our oldest English poet, says,—

"He rode home crown'd with laurel, like a conqueror."

GRATITUDE—*Agrimony.* A sweet, lowly plant, adorned with small, beautiful, golden-coloured flowers, that up-cone like a pile of stars. It is greatly valued by the herb-gatherers in the country, and considered by many to make much better tea than half the rubbish which is sold under that name.

GRIEF or PAIN—*Marigold.* Often alluded to by our ancient poets, as bowing its head and mourning for the absence of the sun.

HAPPY RETIREMENT—*Wild Harebell.* See "Daisy of the Dale," page 100.

HOPE—*Hawthorn.* See Legend of the "Queen of May," page 116, and Poem of "How May was first made," page 129.

HOSPITALITY—*Oak.* In former days the ancients were wont to entertain their guests beneath a tree. Under the oak of Mamre, Abraham welcomed the angels.

HUMILITY—*Broom.* See Legend of "Old Saxon Flowers," pages 50, 51.

ILL-NATURE—*Crab blossom.* "As sour as a crab," has long been an old English saying—hence its signification.

IMMORTALITY—*Amaranth.* One of the flowers which was fabled to grow in the gardens of the gods. Milton mentions it amongst those which blow in heaven, and makes the angels in their adoration cast down

"Their crowns inwove with amaranth and gold:
Immortal amaranth,—a flower which once
In Paradise, fast by the tree of life,
Began to bloom,—but soon, for man's offence,
To heaven removed."

IMPATIENCE—*Balsam.* Which when touched is said to throw the seeds out of the capsules with great force; and from this quality it is selected to express irritation or ingratitude.

INDEPENDENCE—*Wild-plum Blossom.* One of the oldest and hardiest of our English forest fruits, which grows wild in hundreds of hedges, and cannot be trained in gardens or orchards. It seems to love best those rugged and solitary nooks which have never been cultivated by the hand of man since the creation, and is well chosen as an emblem of Independence.

INDIFFERENCE—*Candy-tuft.* So it stands in all floral alphabets, because its blossoms are scentless.

INGRATITUDE—*Buttercup.* So called in the Language of Flowers, because it is supposed to injure the cattle that feed upon it; and no honey can be gathered from the gaudy gold of its flowers: as it is not very likely to figure in a lady's nosegay, we will leave the emblem as it is.

INNOCENCE—*Daisy.* See "Daisy of the Dale," page 99, and Poem, 102.

INSINUATION—*Bindweed*, or *Larger Convolvulus.* Which forces its way through every open space it can find between the branches, until you can scarcely discover another leaf besides its own, so closely are its long, trailing stems twisted along the boughs it has insinuated itself amongst.

LASTING BEAUTY—*Stock*, or *Gillyflower*, for the latter is the old name of this truly English flower, which our ancestors also called July flower It flourished in the gardens of the old baronial castles hundreds of years ago, and time and cultivation have rather added to, than diminished its beauty: and it is, therefore, well deserving of the appellation of Lasting Beauty.

LOVE—*Myrtle.* See Legend of the "Forget-me-Not," page 22.

LOVE'S CAPTIVE—*Peach-blossom.* Every one who has beheld the rich bloom of the Peach must have been captivated by its beauty, whether seen on the velvet cheek of the fruit, or the delicate hue of its blossoms.

MATERNAL LOVE—*Moss.* The soft, green velvet covering of many a spot which would otherwise be brown and barren; it grows around and shelters the stem of many a delicate flower, which would otherwise perish, and gives warmth to many a chilly nook; and so may fancy stretch, link by link, until it traces in it a resemblance to Maternal Love.

MESSAGE—*Iris.* So called from the messenger of Juno, one of the Oceanides; also after the rainbow. Her business seems to have been to cut matters short, and no doubt amongst the young deities of Olympus she often carried the important message of love, and "popped the question." There are about fifty varieties of the Iris.

MODESTY—*Blue Violet.* See "Violet of the Valley," page 33, and "Flowers of Love," page 36.

MUSIC—*Reeds.* Pan, the god of Shepherds, is said to have first formed the Arcadian pipes from Reeds, which he called Syrinx, in honour of a beautiful nymph who was changed into a Reed.

NEGLECTED BEAUTY—*Meadow-sweet.* My predecessors have been pleased to make this beautiful and fragrant flower, which is called the Queen of the Meadow, and whose perfume is sweet as that of the Hawthorn, the emblem of Uselessness. In contradistinction to the meaning they have assigned to it, I have dared to christen it the "Neglected Beauty," for a sweeter flower blows not in all the green meadows of pastoral England, and Neglected Beauty it shall ever represent to me, for it has been too long overlooked. Miss Twamley, in her "Wild Flowers," says — and honour to her for saying it,— "Its tall, red-tinted stems, handsome jagged leaves, and foam-like flowers, so rich in scent, and so very beautiful, well deserve the title so often bestowed upon it of 'Queen of the Meadows.' The French and Italian names have both the same meaning — 'Meadow-Queen.' It fills the summer air with a scent like new-mown hay and hawthorn." Fair readers! shall this sweet flower, so admirably advocated by a lady, any longer stand disgraced as the emblem of Uselessness, or will you not rather step forward and defend it as a Neglected Beauty, until some happier emblem is chosen? Just fancy one of your own sweet selves, for want of an advocate, so thrown back and insulted!

NEGLECTED LOVE — *Laurustinus.* See Legend of the "Forget-me-Not," page 23.

PATIENCE — *Dock.* The haunter of every wayside, where it flourishes in spite of the dust and footsteps that trample it down.

PEACE — *Olive-branch.* One of the oldest emblems on record.

PENSIVENESS — *Cowslip.* Called by our old poets the Sweet Nun of the Fields, and immortalised in Shakspeare's "Midsummer's Night's Dream," where, speaking of Titania, he says,—

"The Cowslips tall her pensioners be;
In their gold coats spots you see:
Those be rubies, fairy favours,
In those freckles live their savours."

under the transparent leaves of the Hazel, for there they will soon become reconciled. Another good method is to join a Nutting party in Autumn, for it is a very old saying, "Many nuts many marriages;" this old amusement, no doubt, having done much towards match-making.

REFUSAL — *Snapdragon*. So called from the closing lips of the flower, which will not open until rudely pressed.

REGRET — *Asphodel*. A flower that in ancient times was planted around the graves of the dead, and was also supposed to grow in the gardens of Elysium. Its real signification is, regret and sorrow for the dead.

REPOSE — *Convolvulus*. See Legend of the "Queen of May," page 126.

RETURN OF HAPPINESS — *Lily of the Valley*. See Legend of "How the Rose became Red," page 67.

RICHES — *Corn*. The most usual representation of wealth.

RUDENESS — *Bur*. It is a favourite amusement amongst country girls to pelt their rustic swains with the bur-dock, and that coat must be very threadbare to which they will not adhere. It is a rude and rustic way of making love.

SADNESS — *Withered Leaves*. An apt emblem in love as well as in nature, telling us that the beauty and brightness of summer are departed.

SEPARATION—*A Sprig of the Rose-tree, from which the bud is plucked.*

SILENCE — *White Rose*. See "Flowers of Thought," page 77.

SIMPLICITY—*White Rosebud*. A chaste and beautiful emblem of simple innocence.

SINCERITY—*Fern.* See Legend of the "Daisy of the Dale," page 101.

SNARE or DECEIT—*Catchfly.* This white flower may be found in almost every sandy field in June; and many a poor fly that is attracted to it by its odour, finds death amid its entangling leaves.

SOLITUDE—*Heath.* See "Flowers of Thought," page 78.

SORROW—*Yew.* One of the oldest monuments that our ancestors erected above the dead.

SYMPATHY—*Thrift.* A good old English name, which means more than can be expressed in half-a-dozen words, and ought never to be forgotten by young lovers; for thriftiness brings comfort, independence, and everything which, with love, makes life happy; and should misfortune come, it meets with more sympathy than idleness and extravagance.

TASTE—*Fuchsia.* See Legend of the "Daisy of the Dale," page 101.

THOUGHT—*Pansy.* So called by Shakspeare, and put into the mouth of that "Rose of May," the fair Ophelia, who says,—

"There's Pansies, that's for thoughts."

See Legend of "Flowers of Thought," page 74.

TIME—*White Poplar.* The ancients traced in it a resemblance to Time, because its leaves are dark on one side and bright on the other; and for this they selected it as the emblem of day and night.

TIMIDITY—*Sensitive Plant.* A flower so delicate that it shrinks from the touch, and shuns even the strong light of day, only expanding in its full beauty towards the cool of the evening. There are two or three varieties of this flower; one of which bears full, round, pink blossoms, another white, and a third yellow. Shelley has immortalised the sensitive plant in one of his most beautiful poems.

TIES OF LOVE—*Tendrils of Climbing Plants.* Called by the French, in floral language, "The Chains of Love."

TRUTH—*The Wild Hyacinth,* or *Bluebell of Spring.* The universal favourite of both old and young, that lights up the dark recesses of the forest, and looks as if a blue cloud had fallen from the face of heaven, and was sleeping there. It is the earliest spring flower that bears old England's favourite colour of "true blue."

UNCONSCIOUS BEAUTY—*Mignionette.* A flower whose sweetness all have inhaled. It is linked to a long sentence in the Language of Flowers, and made to express "Your qualities surpass your charms." But I have preferred making this little darling the emblem of Unconscious Beauty, as equally expressive in the sense, and more emblematical of so sweet and lowly a flower.

UNITED—*Lancaster Rose.* Associated with history, and the union that took place between the rival houses of York and Lancaster, after the peace of England had so long been broken by their wars.

YOUR LOOKS FREEZE ME—*Ice-plant.* A most expressive emblem.

YOUTHFUL HOPE—*Snowdrop.* In distinction to the Hawthorn, which is the old emblem of Hope, I have associated the Snowdrop with Youth, as it is the first flower which blows upon the edge of winter.

YOUTHFULNESS—*Crocus.* Endeared to us as one of the first flowers that breaks through the prison-house of winter, throwing a golden light upon our garden borders like the earliest sunshine of spring. It is well chosen as the emblem of Youth.

FLOWERS

AND THEIR

EMBLEMATIC SIGNIFICATIONS.

Acacia	Elegance.
Acanthus	Arts.
Agrimony	Gratitude.
Amaranth	Immortality.
Andromeda	Pity.
Apple-blossom	Preference.
Apricot-blossom	Doubt.
Asphodel	Regret.
Balsam	Impatience.
Bindweed	Insinuation.
Blackthorn	Difficulty.
Bluebottle	Delicacy.
Bramble	Envy.
Broom	Humility.
Bur	Rudeness.
Buttercup	Ingratitude.
Candy-tuft	Indifference.
Canterbury-bell	Constancy.
Catchfly	Deceit.
Convolvulus	Repose.
Corn	Riches.
Cowslip	Pensiveness.
Crab-blossom	Ill-nature.
Crocus	Youthfulness.
Crown Imperial	Power.
Daisy	Innocence.
Daisy, Michaelmas	After-thought.
Dandelion	Foresight.
Deadly Nightshade	Falsehood.
Dock	Patience.
Eglantine, or *Sweet-Brier* . . .	Poetry.

Fern	Sincerity.
Forget-me-Not	Forget me not.
Fuchsia	Taste.
Gorse	Anger.
Harebell	Happy Retirement.
Hawthorn	Hope.
Hazel	Reconciliation.
Heath	Solitude.
Heliotrope	Devoted Attachment.
Honeysuckle, or *Woodbine*	Devoted Affection.
Hyacinth	Truth.
Ice-Plant	Your looks freeze me.
Iris	Messenger.
Ivy	Friendship.
Jasmine, White	Amiableness.
Jonquil, White	Desire.
Laurel	Glory.
Laurustinus	Neglected Love.
Lilac	First Emotions of Love.
Lily of the Valley	Return of Happiness.
Love-lies-Bleeding	Desertion.
Marigold	Grief or Pain.
Meadow-sweet	Neglected Beauty.
Mignionette	Unconscious Beauty.
Moss	Maternal Love.
Myrtle	Love.
Nettle, stinging	Cruelty.
Oak	Hospitality.
Olive-branch	Peace.
Orange-blossom	Chastity.
Pansy	Thought.
Passion-flower	Belief.
Peach-blossom	Love's Captive.
Pimpernel	Assignation, or Change.
Pink	Pure Love.
Poppy	Consolation.
Primrose	Forsaken.

Reeds	Music.
Rose	Beauty.
Rose, Lancaster	Union.
Rose, Maiden's Blush	Bashfulness.
Rose, White	Silence.
Rosebud, Moss	Confession of Love.
Rosebud, White	Simplicity.
Rosemary	Remembrance.
Sage	Esteem.
Sensitive Plant	Timidity.
Snapdragon	Refusal.
Snowdrop	Youthful Hope.
Sprig of the Rose, flowerless	Separation.
Stock, or *Gillyflower*	Lasting Beauty.
Sweet Pea	Pleasure.
Tendrils of Climbing Plants	Ties of Love.
Thorn Apple	Deceitful Charms.
Thrift	Sympathy.
Tulip	Declaration of Love.
Valerian, Red	Accommodating Disposition.
Vervain	Enchantment.
Violet, Blue	Modesty.
Violet, White	Candour.
Wallflower	Fidelity in Misfortune.
Water-lily, White	Purity of Heart.
White Poplar	Time.
Wild-plum Blossom	Independence.
Wild Strawberry	Perfection.
Willow	Disappointed Love.
Withered Leaves	Sadness.
Wormwood	Absence.
Yellow Day Lily	Coquetry.
Yew	Sorrow.

Thomas Harrild, Printer, Shoe Lane, Fleet Street, London.

www.ingramcontent.com/pod-product-compliance
Lightning Source LLC
Chambersburg PA
CBHW030127030726
47498CB00007B/2582

* 9 7 8 3 3 3 7 8 1 6 2 7 8 *